THE GOSPEL
IN THE
OLD TESTAMENT

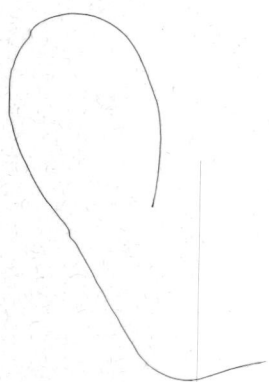

THE GOSPEL
IN THE
OLD TESTAMENT

by
DON BRANDEIS

BAKER BOOK HOUSE
Grand Rapids 6, Michigan
1962

Library of Congress Catalog Card Number: 60-15711

Printed in the United States of America

To

a Mother who, although she cannot see the beauty of Jesus in the Torah, raised me up to be an American and a believer in God. . . .

and to

a Rabbi who taught me to put the study of the Bible first in my life and encouraged me to study for the rabbinate. . . .

and to

a boy named David Swanson who asked to become my brother and who has become a brother indeed. . . .

and to

The Honorable W. May Walker family who took me as a son when the role of being a son was very important in life. . . .

and to

my pastor, Harold G. Sanders, and his wife, June, who were the very first to send me on my evangelistic ministry and ultimate happiness. . . .

and to

a very wonderful physician, J. Lloyd Massey, and his wife, Mary, who have accepted me as a disciple of Jesus and a man with a mission. . . .

and to

Elizabeth Terry who gave me my very first home as a Christian and has kept her love towards me. . . .

and finally to

a loving, living God who saved a man from terrible sin and a ship-wrecked life and who guided his steps to the highest calling in the world — that of being a simple and faithful transmitter for the Light of the World,

I dedicate this book

CONTENTS

INTRODUCTION

It has been the author's express desire to write a manuscript dealing with the Old Testament view of Christianity. This completed work is not to be construed to be wholly a book of theology, for many of the subjects covered are treated for their value but not presented dogmatically. However, I have long been of the opinion that the average minister of the gospel, as well as seminary student, is constantly reviewing the Old Testament solely through the eyes of New Testament Gospels and Pauline pronouncements. Having studied Old Testament history and the Hebrew language for eight years, and having seen the enigma of Jesus Christ revealed through the Torah and the Prophets, it has been the sincere prayer of my heart that I be given grace by our Teacher to put on paper some of the revelations of the Old Testament usually obscured and untested in Judaica-Christianity, yet revelations so powerfully beautiful and commanding to the intellect and imagination that they pour forth new life to those who have ears to hear.

We will do well to remember that God himself is the final authority, guide and revelator. We must transmit His Word—not author it. As believers we search for divine truth in the inspired Scriptures. New light is shed only as the Holy Spirit directs. We cling to and drink from these matchless truths, these wonderful and mysterious utterings through study and meditation under the leadership of the Holy Spirit whose appointed office in the blessed Trinity is to teach the established Word of God.

The Holy Spirit will not—indeed cannot—reveal new doctrines, theologies and so-called revelations that are contrary to the Divine Library. History is the story—yea, the process—of changing man *not* changing God. God has always been the same. True, progressive revelation is a self-evident fact; but let the minister and student well remember that it is man who has changed and not God. Anthropologically speaking, man has regressed, and not evolved, as suggested by many serious men. In this regression man lost sight of the reality of knowing God. Man became worse than beastly in his insane desire to build a world without God as the Maker. Some of earth's children have made the half-way step back to a Divine encounter by a theological approach to their problems. Others have developed a philosophical attitude or code. Actually, it takes both systems of logic, and both systems are magnificently displayed in the Bible.

This book has been written to foster the desire to study more diligently the Divine Library. Along with other books that have dealt with revelation may it be used to stimulate sound thinking, a good evangelical faith full of wisdom and zeal according to the Knowledge of the Most High as revealed through His final source of truth—Jesus Christ.

DON BRANDEIS

Evangelist's Study
Tallahassee, Florida

The Old Testament and...

1

The Existence of God

THE EXISTENCE OF GOD

What profound theology is couched in the very first statement recorded by Moses in Genesis: "In the beginning God created ..." (Genesis 1:1).

The existence of the universe presupposes a Creator. Before a bridge is constructed, it must be conceived in the mind of the architect. The inventor must precede his invention. The universe is indeed an invention, a creation, a vast system of organized galaxies forming a stupendous unity. The celestial spheres disclose a harmonious organization effected by a single mind, without the discords resulting from opposing wills. Before the universe was created, it must of necessity have first been conceived in an infinite mind, for no finite man can create, or as Webster's dictionary puts it, "bring into being from nothing: cause to exist." The Creator must of necessity precede His creation. This self-evident truth was expressed by the divinely inspired Psalmist when he said: "Before the mountains were brought forth, or ever thou hadst formed the earth and the world, even from everlasting to everlasting, thou art God" (Psalm 90:2).

There are those who tell us that they do not believe in the existence of God, simply because no one has ever seen such a being. In other words, they would have us think that they believe only in that which they have the ability to see. However, human experience daily teaches us that we actually believe a great many things which we do not see or understand. Take, for instance, gravitation, electricity, air, thought. No one has ever seen these forces and yet we know that they exist, because of what they do and accomplish. The Scripture says: "The heavens declare the glory of God; and the firmament showeth His handiwork" (Psalm 19:1).

That is to say, as we view His created works we may clearly see and understand that there must be an invisible Being, namely, God, who has brought all these things into existence. For example, we understand that there is a skywriter in the clouds when we see the skywriting, even though our limited senses may be unable to penetrate the distance and see the one who does the writing. In both cases it would be inexcusable to disbelieve.

*   *   *

There is much evidence in the universe for belief in God. There is such abundant and conclusive evidence in the universe of the existence of a Supreme Being, that no unbiased person can consistently deny it. The sublime pageant of the heavenly bodies in their orderly march through infinite space, testifies of the great Architect. Says the prophet: "Lift up your eyes on high, and behold who hath created these things, that bringeth out their host by number: He calleth them all by names by the greatness of His might, for that He is strong in power; not one faileth" (Isaiah 40:26).

Our finite minds are incapable of comprehending the vastness of the universe. Astronomers tell us that all the grains of sand on the beaches of the world would scarcely equal the number of the stars in the universe. Harlow Shapley, Dean of American astronomers, estimates that there are two hundred billion galaxies or island universes, each of which contains billions of stars or suns. All these stars are in perpetual motion. Countless billions of these blazing suns plow their way through limitless space, orbit intersecting orbit like the links of a chain—and yet there is no conflict, no collision! What mathematical Genius has conceived, and planned, made and co-ordinated all these worlds?

"The fool hath said in his heart, There is no God" (Psalm 14:1). Such a one may ascribe the existence of this infinitely complex universe to chance; but chance cannot invent, organize, or plan. Chance cannot even make a watch. Each little wheel, spring, jewel, or cog in the watch has its place. Were we to place the parts of a watch—its jewels, wheels, and springs—in a container, and shake them together ever so vigorously for a million years, those parts would never of themselves make a watch. Only an experienced mind, and skilled hands can fit those parts together. A prominent business man, a manufacturer of cutlery, who had been delivered from the soul-destroying influence of skepticism, and who became a firm and ardent believer in the existence of God, was asked to give one reason for his strong and unyielding faith in the God of the Bible. His answer was as follows:

"It takes a girl in our factory about two days to learn to put the seventeen parts of an electric can opener together. It may be that these millions of worlds, each with its separate orbit, all balanced so wonderfully in space—it may be that they just happened; it may be that by a billion years of tumbling about they finally arranged themselves. I don't know, I am merely a plain manufacturer of can openers. But this I do know, that you can shake the seventeen parts of an electric can opener around in a washtub for the next seventeen billion years and you'll never make an electric can opener."

Doctor Compton, nationally known physicist, believes in God, and assures us that his faith is a very real thing to him. Answering his own question as to what faith is, he says: "For myself, faith begins with the realization that a Supreme Intelligence brought the universe into being and created man. It is not difficult for me to have this faith, for it is incontrovertible that where there is a plan there is intelligence—and an orderly, unfolding universe testifies to the truth of the most majestic statement ever uttered: '*In the beginning, God . . . .*' When man achieves this faith he finds a key to greater happiness and progress."

How the great Creator who upholds these unnumbered worlds in their trackless course, can at the same time give thought, guidance, care, and protection to beings on this tiny world of ours, is beyond all comprehension, but true nevertheless. Says David the Psalmist: "When I consider thy heavens, the work of thy fingers, the moon and the stars, which thou hast ordained; What is man, that thou art mindful of him? and the son of man, that thou visitest him? For thou hast made him a little lower than the angels, and hast crowned him with glory and honor" (Psalm 8:3-5).

Is not such a Creator and Benefactor worthy of our worship, and love?

*   *   *

Our little world abounds in proof of the existence of God. For example, there are laws which determine the weather, the climate, and the seasons. Inexorable law reigns in plant and animal life, in chemistry and physics. There are laws governing light, color, and sound. Design, and symmetry are discernible in every flower, leaf and blade of grass.

Take, for example, the corn on the cob. Did you know that its longitudinal rows are always even in number, either eight, ten, twelve, or fourteen, etc? You will never find an ear of corn having an odd number of such rows. Inanimate nature cannot count. Who then could have planned such an arrangement, if not the mind of the Infinite One?

Consider the tiny snow crystals, with their graceful whorls, the delicately chiseled and beveled edges that decorate them, and their curious dots and loops, are arranged in perfect order about one center. How can one explain the fact that snowflakes are almost always hexagon in shape—either six-sided or six-rayed? Wilson A. Bentley, an authority on snowflakes, and pioneer of snow crystal photography, photographed many thousands of flakes and never found two that were exactly alike! Numberless snowflakes, each with a different design!

Skillful artists and designers use snow crystal photographs for their patterns and creations; jewelers use them for gem-cutting and for designing jewelry and filigree work; workers in art-metal for making decorative ornamental work; scientists, to study the weather, the clouds, and the snow. Lovers of beauty revel in their symmetrical and fragile loveliness.

When he is asked for an explanation of the transcendent beauty of these crystals, Intelligence answers, "Only the Artist who designed and fashioned them knows how it is done."

It matters not whether we study a distant sun through the telescope, or a minute cell through the microscope, we will find the law of design, and purpose pervading every atom in infinite space, including the protons and electrons in the greatest suns and planets in distant space. Wherever creation exists, there must of necessity be a creator. Many sincerely motivated scientists agree that it is impossible to explain the essence and behavior of nature aside from God. One renowned scientist says: "It is pretty clear that no matter what electricity is, it seems to be the ultimate essence of what everything is made of, and by which most processes occur."

"And what is that ultimate essence itself?" you may ask.

"We have our theories," answers every true scientist, "but can't prove them."

In high school my favorite physics teacher told me once as he picked up a bar of magnet, "Bring this near the steel needle, and the needle will leap to the magnet. No one knows why, but we have worked out elaborate explanations. We speak of lines of force; we draw a diagram of the magnetic field. We know there are no lines there, and field is just a word to cover up our ignorance."

He laid the magnet over a wooden base in which was embodied another bar magnet. Immediately the upper bar magnet remained suspended in space about half an inch above the base.

What supports it? Sir Oliver Lodge says it is the all-pervading ether. But Einstein denies that there is any ether. Which is right? I say that the magnet repels another magnet by the will of God. And no man today can give a more precise answer....

William Ritter, former director of the Scripps Institution for Biological Research, University of California, says: "Seeing God in the universe is no more difficult than seeing electrons there"; while Pasteur, French scientist and father of bacteriology, declared: "Posterity will one day laugh at the sublime foolishness of the materialistic philosophy. The more I study nature the more I stand amazed at the work of the Creator. I pray at work in my laboratory."

Kircher, the celebrated astronomer, had an acquaintance who was an infidel, whom he wished to convince of the existence of the Creator. In order to do this, he procured a beautiful globe with its revolving satellites. Just before his skeptic friend entered the room, Kircher wound up the device and set it in motion. After looking admiringly at it for a while, the skeptic inquired, "Who made that?" Kircher answered him in his own currency: "No one made it. It came into existence by mere chance. It was doubtlessly produced by resident forces." "Nonsense!" answered the skeptic. He was soon reminded of the fact that he had convicted himself.

"No man," said Professor Moorehouse of Drake University, "can be a lover of astronomy, and an atheist at the same time."

> The spacious firmament on high
> With all the blue ethereal sky,
> And spangled heavens, a shining frame,
> Their great Original proclaim:
> The unwearied sun, from day to day
> Does his Creator's pow'r display,
> And publishes to every land
> The work of an almighty hand.

The wise man counsels: "Go to the ant, thou sluggard; consider her ways, and be wise" (Proverbs 6:6). Who can explain the wonders of animal behavior? Man has invented a word for it. He calls it "instinct." But what is instinct? No one knows. Who has endowed the ant with the superior wisdom that makes it the world's first mining-engineer? Who made it possible for the humble water-spider to be the world's first hydraulic engineer? The waterspider builds its nest under water, fastening it to a rock, log, or stick, with the opening to the nest pointing downward. In order to force the water out of this thimble-sized nest, the spider brings tiny air bubbles into it. It repeats this operation until all the water has been forced out of the nest, and it is ready for the laying of its eggs. Who taught the spider that the air will displace the water in its nest? How was the spider able to discern this scientific fact thousands of years before Archimedes discovered it?

The shell-spider is the world's first civil engineer. It lifts a shell, possibly a hundred times its own weight, to a branch about eighteen inches above the ground. How it performs this feat of engineering is indeed a marvel of marvels! It first turns the shell downward, in order to drain out the water that may be in it; it then spins a web from the shell to the branch. The web shrinks as it dries, and thus lifts the shell a little closer toward the branch. The spider then spins another web, and still another, each strand lifting the shell closer, until the shell is hoisted and fastened to the branch.

Bees are the world's first sanitary engineers. When a mouse enters their hive, they sting it to death; and inasmuch as bees are vegetarians, they do not feed on the carcass. In order to prevent the decaying corpse from contaminating the rest of the beehive, they seal it air-tight with a special wax, and so perfectly is the work done, that not the slightest taint of decay or the faintest odor can seep through it. Who taught these bees and gave them this marvelous wisdom? The same God who bids His children: "Be ye clean."

*   *   *

There is much evidence in the human body to support our contention. Man has within himself a fully equipped I.B.M. machine far exceeding the wonders of the electronic brain with its millions of wires. If the living human body could be magnified a million times, we would behold mysterious processes which would stagger the imagination! We are told that the tissues of our bodies are composed of twenty-eight billions of cells, and that each cell and tissue requires food for metabolism. Does man consciously contribute anything to the accomplishment of this stupendous process? He does not in the slightest degree. All that man does is to partake of food, and to masticate it. The stomach, the intestines, the liver, the nerves, the heart, the blood, the lymph do the rest. The blood delivers the nourishment to each of these twenty-eight billion cells, and the body does the rest, forming bone, nerve, and muscle. Strange as it may seem, the stomach knows more about food than does man himself. How frequently it ejects unwholesome food, as if in violent protest against the abuse!

It is fascinating to observe how quickly the body counteracts disease when some kind of disturbance occurs. An alarm is immediately sent out from the nerve center in the brain, at once setting in motion new activities in the body in its effort to overcome the difficulty. Swarms of white cells are quickly manufactured in the marrow of the bones, and these cells go forth to prevent any further intrusion of the invading germ. Restorative forces are at work, and healing has begun. Where does the human body obtain this power to repair itself? In the words of Scripture: "Who hath put wisdom in the inward parts? or who hath given understanding to the heart?" (Job 38:36).

In an address before the annual meeting of the Massachusetts Medical Society, June 1, 1937, on "The Wisdom of the Body," and reported by the *New England Journal of Medicine,* November 18, 1937, Dr. R. C. Cabot, Dean of Boston Physicians, and Emeritus Professor of Clinical Medicine, Harvard Medical School, enumerated many of the mysterious functions and processes of the body which no scientist understands or can explain, particularly those forces and processes that are summed up in the term, "The Healing Power of Nature."

"But what is Nature?" he asked. "What are the characteristics of this power? The first is that of its *superhuman* wisdom. Where does this force come from? Where do we get the healing substance in our tissue? I do not see why we should not call it by its natural name....It is perfectly obvious that it is God. It is the power of God upon which each one here depends today, for the fact that he is here instead of being underneath the earth....The medical profession has learned in studying disease, more about the meaning of this word [God] than the vast majority of the so-called religious people. Why not tell this truth, because it is true?"

The human eye is a marvelous photographic camera, constantly sending picture messages to the brain. The ear is a supersensitized sound apparatus, capable of recognizing a familiar voice among a thousand. And what might not be said of the nervous system, with its millions of tiny nerve endings and shoots reaching every part of the body, carrying messages to the human mind, of man's personality, and destiny? Is it any wonder the inspired Psalmist exclaimed: "I am fearfully and wonderfully made"? (Psalms 139:14).

Since He bestowed so much thought in the creation of man, is it reasonable to suppose that God will neglect to care for him? Are you at times tempted to think God does not care—that He has forgotten you? Listen to what He has to say concerning this: "Can a women forget her sucking child, that she should not have compassion on the son of her womb? yea, they may forget, yet will I not forget thee" (Isaiah 49:15).

The Bible tells us clearly that God is a real, personal Being. It declares that God has personal attributes. We quote: "And the Lord passed by before him [Moses], and proclaimed, The Lord, The Lord God, *merciful and gracious, longsuffering, and abundant in goodness and truth, Keeping mercy for thousands,* forgiving iniquity and transgression and sin, and that will by no means clear the guilty" (Exodus 34:6, 7). Only a personal God can possess such attributes.

*   *   *

God daily, in a hundred and one ways, demonstrates His love and mercy towards His creatures. The marvelous adaptation of nature to the needs of mankind is an expression of God's love. Every meal that we partake of and enjoy, should declare to us that "God is love." Each flower with its beautiful tints and delicate fragrance speaks to us that "God is love." Each bird that makes the air alive with its happy song, proclaims that "God is love." The blue heavens, the warm sunshine, the refreshing rain, the glorious sunsets, the innumerable material blessings which are ours every day, all testify to the fact that "God is love."

But nature, marred as it is by the effects of sin, does not perfectly represent the character of God. Many today are drifting along, without chart or compass, troubled and frustrated, knowing neither peace of heart nor rest of soul, and all because they have never learned to know Him "who is the health of my countenance" (Psalm 42:11). Many there are whose language is like that of the afflicted Job: "Oh that I knew where I might find Him!" (Job 23:3).

Beloved, is this your heart-cry? Do you long to know Him who is "the chiefest among ten thousand," and "altogether lovely"? (See Song of Solomon 5:10, 16.) Is it your heart's desire to become acquainted with the One whose marvelous works in earth, sea, and sky speak so eloquently and persistently that "God is love"? Listen:

You may have a daily rendezvous with your heavenly Father in the life of His Son—the holy Child of Bethlehem. Whatever may be your condition, your dilemma, or perplexity, or your uncertainty, there is help for you in the Bible. Its message will be a soothing influence to your troubled heart. There you will find comfort, and only there will you find rest. So let God speak to you through his Holy Spirit. Let Him whisper His secrets to you personally, and as you reach out, you will better understand His loving plans and purposes for you. Then, as your soul is lifted above the daily sorrows and frustrations, into a realm of peace, you too will be able to say from experience that, "God is love." Therefore: "Acquaint now thyself with him, and be at peace: thereby good shall come unto thee" (Job 22: 21).

2

The Fall of Man

By yielding to the evil insinuations of the enemy, man broke the commandments which say, "Thou shalt not covet," and "Thou shalt not steal." Thus sin—which is the transgression of the law—was introduced into the world, and man became the servant of Satan, the originator of sin.

*   *   *

After Adam and Eve transgressed God's command, their eyes were indeed opened—opened to discern their folly. The accusing spirit of Satan now took possession of them, and they cast the blame upon one another, and upon their Creator. "The woman whom thou gavest to be with me," said Adam, "she gave me of the tree, and I did eat" (Genesis 3:12). And Eve said, "The serpent beguiled me, and I did eat" (Genesis 3:13). This spirit of self-justification which originated in Lucifer, the father of lies; was indulged in by Adam and Eve as soon as they yielded to Satan's influence, and it was displayed when God confronted them with their sin. It has been manifested ever since. Folks try to shield themselves by casting the blame upon others, upon circumstances, or even upon God Himself.

As a penalty for his sin, man was to return to the ground from whence he was taken: "for dust thou art, and unto dust shalt thou return" (Genesis 3:19). Because of sin, a curse rested upon the earth (Genesis 3:17), and death became the lot of the human family. Lest sin should be perpetuated, and man become immortal by partaking of the tree of life after his fall, "the Lord God sent him forth from the garden of Eden. . . . So he drove out the man; and he placed at the east of the garden of Eden cherubim, and a flaming sword which turned every way, to keep the way of the tree of life" (Genesis 3:23, 24). The Bible plainly teaches that man is mortal by nature, and any system of religion which teaches otherwise, is but reiterating Satan's lie: "Ye shall not surely die" (Genesis 3:4).

The disobedience of Adam and Eve opened the floodgates of sin and transgression upon the world. Our first parents soon perceived in their children and in nature about them the terrible results of their disobedience. The swelling tide of evil and wickedness with its suffering, pain, and death could not be stayed. It increased and multiplied, until, as recorded in the Sacred Scriptures: "God saw that the wickedness of man was great in the earth, and that every imagination of the thoughts of his heart was only evil continually" (Genesis 6:5). God destroyed the antediluvian generation by a flood, but spared Noah and his family.

The same sins that called forth the vengeance of God upon the antediluvian world, exist today. As men refuse to respond to the restraining influence of the Spirit of God, and abandon themselves to the promptings and desires of their sinful, natural heart, the evil results are soon apparent in their lives of greed, vice, strife, and war. It was thus in the early days, and it will ever be so, until God puts an end to sin.

*   *   *

When Adam and Eve heard of the life of toil and sorrow which was to be their portion because of their sin, they also heard words of hope—the promise of a Redeemer—"I will put enmity between thee and the woman, and between thy seed and her seed; it [or he] shall bruise thy head and thou shalt bruise his heel" (Genesis 3:15).

This seed of the woman represents the Messiah, who was to bruise the serpent's head, and bring deliverance from sin and transgression to every believing child of God. Satan, the sworn enemy of man, delights in tempting us to disobey and displease God. And as we reap the bitter consequences of such insane transgression, he urges us to blame it all on God. Inasmuch as Satan is exceedingly more powerful than man, God in His infinite love promised to send the Saviour into the world to conquer this ruthless enemy, and also to enable us to keep the laws which say, "Thou shalt not covet," etc. As we receive this blessed Saviour into our hearts, He will help us to overcome our inherited and cultivated tendencies to do evil, and to form characteristics that reflect God's holiness and will.

In this vigorous battle between the forces of God and Satan there can be no compromise and no neutrality. Everyone must decide between obedience or transgression, between God and Satan. This struggle between these two contending forces takes place in every heart. It is unceasing, and will increase in intensity as we draw near the end of our individual life.

Satan's terrible history of rebellion, his rule and its effects upon man and angels are designed to be a lesson-book through all the coming ages. Although our planet is only a speck in the great universe of God, yet upon it is concentrated the attention of the dwellers of heaven and the demons of hell. It is on this earth that the victory for righteousness, which began in heaven, is to be consummated for all times.

We, today, are witnessing the outworking of Satan's principles, and each one of us is an actor in this drama of the ages, which is to terminate with the coming of the Saviour. As we draw nearer and nearer to the end of the reign of evil, and closer and closer to that day when Jesus shall come to put an end to the dominion of Satan, an intensity will take possession of every earthly element... "affliction shall not rise up the second time" (Nahum 1:9; cf. Ezekiel 28:17-19).

*   *   *

"But why," you may ask, "do good people suffer, and why are they afflicted?" It is because there is a war over every soul. Satan especially hates those who have deserted his ranks and who have joined themselves to God. Satan, called "the accuser of our brethren," accuses "them before our God day and night" (Revelation 12:10; see Zechariah 3:1). He impugns the purity of their motives in serving God. (Read Job, chapters 1 and 2.) In order to vindicate them before the heavenly host, God permits Satan to test them. Were it not for the restraining hand of God, Satan and his demons would destroy the righteous and all that we hold dear in this life. Though the righteous are tested, and tested severely, God overrules and makes all things work together for their good. It is through trial and suffering, through sorrow and affliction, that character is perfected and that the soul is brought in closer contact with its only Source of strength. "When He hath tried me," declared the much afflicted Job, "I shall come forth as gold (Job 23:10).

One day a visitor watched a goldsmith heat the gold in his crucible. The fires grew hotter and hotter. All the while the goldsmith kept his eye on the crucible. Finally the curious inquirer asked: "Why are you watching the gold so intently? What is it that you are looking for?" To which the craftsman replied: *"I am looking for my face.* When I can see myself in the molten gold, then I turn off the heat, for the work is done."

The Master Workman is watching the furnace of your affliction most closely, for He sees something worthwhile in you to perfect; and just as soon as He discerns His own likeness reflected in your character, the affliction will be removed.

We read in the Scriptures that the Hebrews, because of their murmuring and rebellion at God's providences, were bitten by fiery serpents and many of them died as a result. And Moses prayed for the people. And the Lord said unto Moses, "Make thee a fiery serpent, and set it upon a pole: and it shall come to pass, that every one that is bitten, when he looketh upon it, shall live" (Numbers 21:8).

As the Hebrews were bidden to look upon the uplifted serpent and live, so we must look upon Jesus, if we are to be saved from the fatal results of sin, which is eternal damnation and death.

Some time ago a young man was bitten by a dog infected with rabies. Not aware of his great peril, the man left the city for an unknown destination. Newspapers were informed of his case and immediately a message was sent over the radio networks warning this person that unless an antidote was administered at once, he was doomed to die. Fortunately, the message reached the young man in time and his life was saved.

For thousands of years, ever since the fall of Adam, God has been, as it were, broadcasting to the doomed sinner: "Where art thou?" Whoever you are and wherever you are, do you hear your heavenly Father's voice calling you and pleading with you even as He did with his ancient people? Mankind must accept the divine antidote and look to Jesus and live! It is Christ or chaos!

3

The Son of God

THE SON OF GOD

Few names in history are as well known to all peoples, as is the name of Abraham. Millions of Hebrews and countless millions of Christians and Mohammedans hold that name dear. While other renowned characters of antiquity have gone down into oblivion, the name of the patriarch Abraham has lost none of its appeal with the passing of the centuries.

Wherein lies the charm of his personality, the secret of his fascination? Abraham was not a great statesman like Joseph, nor a mighty leader like Moses, nor a general like Joshua. He did not possess the wisdom of a Solomon, nor the genius of David. He did not attain to eminence as an inventor, explorer, or conqueror. How then shall we explain his remarkable hold upon man's imagination during the past three thousand years?

Abraham excelled in one respect. He was a man of great *faith,* and this noble trait of character earned for him the immortal designation of "the father of the faithful." He had unbounded faith in God's *Word.* His was not a blind belief or a mere mental assent. His confidence was based upon knowledge. He *knew* God. He knew that the One who formed this vast universe had all power, and that all resources were at His command and disposal. Why then should he question any statement that Jehovah God might make?

Jehovah promised Abraham that his seed would be as numerous as the stars in the heavens. (See Genesis 15:5.) The faithful patriarch was nearly a hundred years old and childless when this promise was made to him. He could not understand how such a promise could possibly be fulfilled. Had he been so disposed, he would have had ample opportunity to question God's statement. But the inspired Scriptures tell us that "He believed in the Lord: and He [God] counted it to him for righteousness" (Genesis 15:6). "He staggered not at the promise of God through unbelief; but was strong in faith, giving glory to God; And being fully persuaded, that what he had promised, he was able also to perform" (Romans 4:20, 21).

This grand old patriarch did not limit the omnipotence of the Holy One of Israel. It was enough for him that God had spoken, and it was his part to take Him at His word. What an example he left for his posterity to emulate!

Many people find it difficult to believe that Jesus, the Messiah, is the *only* begotten Son of God. They question, "How can God have a son?" But is it for finite man to speculate and question God's power or ability? Why should we attempt to circumscribe God's omnipotent power? The question before all humanity is, What does God say in regard to this matter? Does He or does He not tell us that He has a Son? The Old Testament answers in the affirmative. Text after text, iterates and reiterates this truth; namely, that God has a Son. How then shall we relate ourselves to this revelation? Abraham never doubted God's word; shall we, his seed, do less?

*   *   *

The testimony of Genesis is very clear. In the very first verse of the first chapter of the first book of the Bible—the book of Genesis—Moses informs us that there is more than one person in the Godhead: "In the beginning *Elohim* created the heavens and the earth."

The Hebrew word: *Elohim* literally means Gods. *El* is the singular for God; *Elohim* is the plural. Therefore, the verse rightly translated should read, "In the beginning Gods, or the Godhead, created the heavens and the earth." The word God appears thirty-one times in the first chapter, therefore, we have thirty-one reasons for believing in the plurality of the Godhead.

The first chapter of Genesis also records what God created each day. Concerning the sixth day we read: "And *Elohim* said: Let *us* make man in *our* image, after *our* likeness" (Genesis 1:26).

The plural pronoun *us* is also used in Genesis 3:22 where it says: "And Jehovah *Elohim* said, Behold, the man is become as one of *us.* . . ."

In Genesis 11:6, 7, it is recorded that: "Jehovah said....Go to, let *us* go down, and there confound their language."

Whom was God addressing when He said "Let *us*"? Rashi, the distinguished Jewish commentator, suggests that God was addressing angels. Angels, however, were themselves created; they, therefore, cannot create. Furthermore, the Scripture declares that man was created "in the image of God" (Genesis 1:27). Nowhere in Holy Scriptures is man declared to have been created in the image of *angels*.

* * *

There is clear evidence of a plurality of persons in God's words: "Let *us* make man." The divinely inspired Book of Proverbs like-wise speaks of a plurality of persons active in creation. We quote: "The Lord possessed *me* in the beginning of His way, before His works of old. I was set up from everlasting, from the beginning, or ever the earth was....When He prepared the heavens, I was there ....Then I was by Him, as one brought up with Him..." (Proverbs 8:22-30).

An explanation of this plurality is plainly stated in another chapter of the same book: "Who hath ascended up into heaven, or descended? who hath gathered the wind in his fists? who hath bound the waters in a garment? who hath established all the ends of the earth? what is his name, and *what is his son's name,* if thou canst tell? Every word of God is pure" (Proverbs 30:4, 5).

In this Scripture it is declared that the Son existed with the Father from everlasting, from the days of eternity. This Son was associated with the Father in the creation. In the light of subsequent Scripture we can understand the words: "Let *us* make man."

* * *

Every pious Hebrew quite frequently recites the Shema: "Hear, O Israel: The Lord our God is one Lord" (Deuteronomy 6:4).

It should be noted that in Hebrew the above words "our God" are in reality "our Gods," or *Eloheinu,* with the letter *yod* added, which makes this word plural and not singular. Thus the literal translation of the above text is, "Hear O Israel, Jehovah, our Gods, Jehovah is one *(echad)*."

The Hebrew word *echad* denotes *unity,* rather than *individuality.* Thus, for example, when God gave Adam his wife, He said of them,

"And they shall be *echad* [one flesh]." In this Scripture two are declared to be one—*echad*—a unity. When God made the first day of the week, the record says that it consisted of two parts—evening and morning. Yet the Scripture says, "The evening the morning were *yomechad* [one day]," in other words, a unity. In Ezra 2:64 is found the phrase *kol hakohol ke-echad*—"all the congregation is one" (*echad*)—a unity.

When the Bible speaks of one individual, it uses such terms as *yochid, levado, bilti, ish, prat, boded,* etc., as, for instance in the case of Abraham when God bade him to offer up his only son, Isaac, God said: *Kach no es bincho es yechidcho,*—"Take now thy son, thine only son" (Genesis 22:2). The word *yochid* and not *echad* is used to designate a single individual, but *echad,* a unity.

God unmistakably refers to another divine person when He says in the writings of Moses: "Behold I send an Angel before thee, to keep thee in the way, and to bring thee into the place which I have prepared. Beware of him, and obey his voice, provoke him not; for he will not pardon your transgressions: for my name is in him" (Exodus 23:20, 21).

This Scripture is very illuminating. God informs us that there is a person who bears His name—the name of God—for God says of Him, "My name is in him." This person who has the power to forgive sins, must be divine, for "who can forgive sins but God only?" (Mark 2:7).

In Exodus 14:19, it is declared that this Angel, or Messenger who bears God's name, went before the children of Israel during their sojourn in the wilderness. In Exodus 13:21, we are told that it was the Lord who went before them. In Exodus 3:2 we read that: "The Angel of the Lord appeared unto him [Moses] in a flame of fire out of the midst of a bush."

In verses 4 and 6 we learn that this angel of the Lord is God. We quote: "I am the God of thy father, the God of Abraham, the God of Isaac, and God of Jacob. And Moses hid his face: for he was afraid to look upon God."

Thus we see that this Angel, or Messenger, bears the same family name—God—and that He possesses the same attributes as God.

When the Saviour was here on earth, the writings of Moses had been so grossly misinterpreted by the religious aristocracy that He was impelled to address them in these words of stern rebuke and warning: "Do not think that I will accuse you to the Father: there is one that accuseth you, even Moses, in whom ye trust. For had ye believed Moses, ye would have believed me: for he wrote of me. But if ye believe not his writings, how shall ye believe my words?" (John 5:45-47).

* * *

Furthermore, David, the sweet singer of Israel recognized the plurality in the Godhead, for he wrote by inspiration: "Jehovah said unto my Lord, Sit thou at my right hand, until I make thine enemies thy footstool" (Psalm 110:1).

In this text two divine persons are mentioned: "Jehovah" and "Lord." The Sanhedrin, the Sofrim, and the religious leaders, were familiar with this Scripture, and should have understood its significance.

One day while in conversation with the Pharisees, Jesus referring to this text, asked them: "What think ye of the Messiah? Whose Son is He? They say unto him, The son of David. He saith unto them, How then doth David in spirit call him Lord, saying, The Lord said unto my Lord, Sit thou on my right hand, till I make thine enemies thy footstool? If David then call Him Lord, how is he his son? And no man was able to answer him a word, neither durst any man from that day forth ask him any more questions." (Matthew 22:42-46).

Why was no one able to answer the Saviour's question? It was simply because the Scripture was too plain and self-evident in its declaration that there was more than one person in the divine Unity. The same truth is enunciated in other Psalms, but space will permit us to refer to but one more quotation: "Thy throne, O God, is for ever and ever: the sceptre of Thy kingdom is a right sceptre. Thou lovest righteousness, and hatest wickedness: therefore *God, thy God,* hath anointed thee with the oil of gladness above thy fellows" (Psalm 45:6, 7).

In these verses, one divine person is addressing another divine person. Who is the One addressed? The inspired writer of the book of Hebrews gives us the answer: "But unto the Son He saith, Thy throne, O God, is for ever and ever: a sceptre of righteousness is the sceptre of thy kingdom. Thou hast loved righteousness, and hated iniquity; therefore God, even thy God, hath anointed thee with the oil of gladness above thy fellows" (Hebrews 1:8, 9).

The entire second Psalm forecasts the determined opposition the Saviour, the Son of God, would meet with here on earth, and His ultimate triumph over His enemies. We quote: "The kings of the earth set themselves, and the rulers take counsel together, against the Lord, and against His Anointed. [The Hebrew for "His Anointed" is *Meshicho*—literally "His Messiah."]...I set my king upon my holy hill of Zion. I will declare the decree: the Lord hath said unto me, *Thou art my Son;* this day have I begotten thee.... Kiss the Son, lest he be angry, and ye perish from the way when His wrath is kindled but a little. Blessed are all they that put their trust in *him.*" God has never told us to put our trust in a mere human being, whether it be in David, in Solomon, or in any other person. Indeed, God forbids us to place our confidence in mortal man. He says: "Cursed be the man that trusteth in *man,* and maketh flesh his arm" (Jeremiah 17:5).

God will not ask us to do something in one place which he has expressly forbidden us to do in another place. It must be very evident to any candid, unbiased mind that this second Psalm speaks of a divine person, the King (verse 6), the Saviour (verse 2), the One who eventually will inherit the heathen, and the uttermost parts of the earth for His possession (verse 8), the One who merits our faith and trust (verse 12), the Son of God (verse 7). Blessed indeed is the man who has a firm faith in God and in the wonderful Saviour, His Son, the Lord Jesus.

*   *   *

It is also the unanimous testimony of the ancient prophets, that the One who existed with the Father before this world was created, would take upon Him human form in order to become our Messiah and Redeemer. We quote Isaiah: "For unto us a child is born, unto us a son is given: and the government shall be upon his shoulder: and his name shall be called Wonderful, Counsellor, the Mighty God, the everlasting Father, the Prince of Peace. Of the increase of his government and peace there shall be no end, upon the throne of David, and upon his kingdom, to order it, and to establish it with judgment and with justice from henceforth even for ever" (Isaiah 9:6, 7).

Note the import of these texts—the mighty God, the Prince of Peace, the One whose government was to be an everlasting one, was to be born, was to take upon Himself the form of humanity. A prince is the son of a king. In Daniel 9:25 the Messiah is divine; he is indeed a Prince, the Son of God.

In Isaiah 7:14 the God of Abraham made it known in what manner His Son was to be born. He tells us: "Therefore the Lord himself shall give you a sign; behold a *virgin* shall conceive, and bear a son, and shall call His name *Immanuel* [God with us]."

The Hebrew word for "virgin" here is *al-mah*. Some Jewish commentators suggest that the only correct Hebrew word for a "virgin" is *bthulah*. The Scriptures, however, teach otherwise. In Genesis 24:43, for instance, Rebekah is called *he-almah*—the virgin—before she became Isaac's wife, while in Joel 1:8 a *bthulah* is said to be weeping for the *husband* of her youth.

Many of earth's children find it difficult to believe, and hard to understand how the Saviour could possibly have been born without a human father, but "Is anything too hard for the Lord?" (Genesis 18:14).

God tells us in the above Scripture, Isaiah 7:14, that He would give us a sign in order that we may have no difficulty in identifying the true Messiah. In the Bible a sign is synonymous with a wonder or a miracle. (See Exodus 4:8, 9, 17, 21). God designed that the Saviour's manner of birth should be miraculous, supernatural, different from that of any ordinary human being, yes, contrary to all the laws of nature.

What shall be our position toward this simple, pointed testimony of Scripture? Shall we believe only that which our finite minds can comprehend and understand? Is the power of God to be circumscribed by our human limitations? Was not Isaac a miracle child? And did not God create Adam from the dust of the ground without father or mother? Surely the same God who created man out of the dust of the ground, is fully able to fulfil His promise of a miraculous birth for His only-begotten Son.

* * *

On numerous occasions Jesus stated that He was the divine Son of God. In John 3:16 He declared Himself to be "the only-begotten Son" of God.

In John 10:30 He says, "I and my Father are one." In Matthew 3:16, 17 it is recorded that a voice from heaven declared Him to be the Son of God. He demonstrated His divine Sonship by raising the dead (John 5:21; 11:41-45), and pointed to His mighty miracles as undeniable evidence of His divinity. (See John 14:10, 11.) His disciples acknowledged Him as the Messiah, the divine Son of God. (See Matthew 16:16; John 6:69.) His bitterest enemies could not help but concede that He possessed miracle-working power. (See John 11:47, 48.) And even inanimate nature recognized Him as its

Master and carried out His commands, for we read that "even the winds and the sea obey Him" (Matthew 8:27).

God's great sacrifice in offering up His only-begotten Son reveals a love which passes all understanding. Earth's race has broken God's eternal and immutable law and holiness, and only one who is God could atone for its transgression. There was no other way, therefore, to save man from the penalty of death than by the death of a divine substitute.

In order to impress this profound truth upon the heart of Abraham and upon all mankind, the aged patriarch was subjected to the closest test that man was ever called upon to endure—that of offering up his only son, Isaac, whom he loved, for a burnt offering. So implicit was Abraham's confidence in God, so deep his love for Him, that he did not shrink from this supreme sacrifice. In consenting to offer up his only son, Abraham had a foretaste of our heavenly Father's experience when *He* offered up *His* beloved Son as an atonement for our sins; but with this exception: no pitying hand was extended to stay the execution of God's beloved Son! God's Son drank the cup to its bitter dregs and endured without a murmur or complaint, the mockery, the abuse, and the sufferings and agonies which are the inevitable accompaniment of death by horrible crucifixion. What infinite, unfathomable love for a world that did not love Him!

*   *   *

Here is also the testimony of the Roman soldier concerning the Saviour. Among these who witnessed the sufferings of the Son of God on the cross was a Roman soldier, a centurion. He beheld the bruised body of the Saviour, His hands and His feet lacerated by the spikes. He heard the Prince of Sufferers plead with the Father, "Father, forgive them, for they know not what they do." Even in His dying agony the great heart of the Son of God went out to His persecutors, who were in so great need of pardon and redeeming grace. The centurion's heart was profoundly moved by this evidence of the Reedemer's divinity and he exclaimed, "Truly, this was the Son of God" (Matthew 27:54).

And, indeed, who can contemplate the death of Jesus with stoical indifference? What infinite value God must place upon each one of us to pay such a staggering price for our redemption! Can we henceforth doubt the Father's love for us?

A story is told about two lads, Larry and Jimmy, who became friends overseas, while in the service of their country, during World War II. Larry was the son of a prominent financier. One day he gave Jimmy a note and said, "Take this, just in case something happens to me; and if you are ever in any difficulty, look up my dad." Shortly afterwards, Larry was fatally wounded in battle.

After the war, Jimmy like many other veterans, was without employment, and his courage was at a low ebb. In his extremity he thought of his dead buddy's note and decided to call on his father who was living in Miami, Florida. He presented Larry's letter which read, "Dad, this will introduce Jimmy, my buddy. Please help him for my sake. Your son, Larry."

As he read his son's familiar handwriting, the financier's face softened, and tears flowed freely down his cheeks. Overcome with emotion, he threw his arms about the young man and in a voice choked with tears, he said, "Jimmy, for my son Larry's sake, you shall from now on be as one of the family."

We, too, have a Friend—the Son of God, whose Father is fabulously rich, for all the boundless resources of the vast universe are His. Said the Saviour, "No man cometh unto the Father, but by me" (John 14:6). The Son bids us call on His Father in any emergency and says reassuringly: "Verily, verily, I say unto you, Whatsoever ye ask the Father in my name, he will give it you. Hitherto have ye asked nothing in my name; ask, and ye shall receive, that your joy may be full" (John 16:23, 24). And to encourage our asking, the Son of God adds: "The Father himself loveth you, because ye have loved me, and have believed that I came out from God" (John 16:27).

Then ask, and you shall not ask in vain, for as you come to the Father in the name of His Son, a royal welcome awaits you. The Father will encircle you in the arms of His love and receive you as His very own. He will do for you infinitely more than you can ask or think. If you will ask Him to forgive your sins, He will grant your request for His Son's sake, and cleanse you from all unrighteousness. His eternal security will be your portion. You will receive power to cast off the harsh shackles of sin and to resist the madness of the evil one, for "If the Son...shall make you free, ye shall be free indeed" (John 8:36). Through faith in Jesus, the Son of God, you will become Abraham's spiritual seed and joint-heir with him to whom God promised the whole world for his possession. In accepting Him as our Saviour and Redeemer "Then are ye Abraham's seed and heirs according to the promise" (Galatians 3:29).

Let the whole Adamic race shout with joy over this victory and elevation.

4

The Birth of Jesus

THE BIRTH OF JESUS

Astronomers, as well as all thoughtful observers are impressed with the mathematical accuracy of the starry heavens. The universe is made after the manner of an immense clock; the Creator of all things does things according to His own schedule. Professor Harlow Shapley, Director of the Harvard Observatory of Cambridge, Massachusetts, under the auspices of the "Society of Arts" of the Massachusetts Institute of Technology has stated that this planet runs with minute precision, even though it is but a mere speck in God's great universe. All the starry galaxies, the island universes, the myriads of suns, the unnumbered worlds, move in their appointed orbits with the same mathematical precision. The Creator bids us contemplate this glorious spectacle of the heavens when He says: "Lift up your eyes on high, and behold who hath created these things, that bringeth out their host by number: he calleth them all by names by the greatness of his might, for that he is strong in power; not one faileth" (Isaiah 40:26).

The wise seer said: "To every thing there is a season, and a time to every purpose under the heaven" (Ecclesiastes 3:1.) Whatever God undertakes to do, He accomplishes on time. There are no bounds to God's ability to carry out His designs, for all the resources of the universe are at His command. His facilities are immeasurable and limitless. "Ah, Lord God!" exclaimed one of Israel's prophets, "behold thou hast made the heaven and the earth by thy great power and stretched out arm, and there is nothing too hard for thee" (Jeremiah 32:17). Whatever God predetermines to do in heaven or on earth, He is fully able to perform without deferment or delay. In all His works perfect accuracy and minute precision may be seen.

We learn from the Scriptures that God revealed through His word the exact time of the Messiah's appearing. This particular prophecy is found in the ninth chapter of the book of Daniel, and deals with days, weeks, and years. It has been said that "figures do not lie." God has not left so important a subject as the Saviour's coming to conjecture or guesswork. He invites us to figure out this prediction for ourselves and then to base our faith on the evidence thus presented. We need not remain doubting Thomases. If we are seeking for proof, it is our privilege to examine the data given us, and then form our conclusions accordingly.

About the year 606 B.C., Nebuchadnezzar, king of Babylon, conquered Judea, destroyed the temple, and carried many of the Hebrews captive into Babylon. It had previously been revealed to the prophet Jeremiah that this captivity was to last seventy years. (See Jeremiah 25:11, 12.) At the expiration of this period, the Jews were to have the privilege of returning to their fatherland.

Among the exiled Hebrews who were taken to Babylon, was Daniel the statesman-prophet. Daniel was familiar with the writings of the prophet Jeremiah, and as the seventy-year captivity drew near to its close, Daniel prayed to God that the promised restitution might be realized. The prophet most earnestly pleaded that Abraham's offspring be given another opportunity to live up to their exalted privileges as God's chosen people. He prayed: "O Lord, according to all thy righteousness, I beseech thee, let thine anger and thy fury be turned away from thy city Jerusalem, thy holy mountain: because for our sins, and for the iniquities of our fathers, Jerusalem and thy people are become a reproach to all that are about us....O, Lord hear; O Lord, forgive; O, Lord, hearken and do; defer not, for thine own sake, O my God: for thy city and thy people are called by thy name" (Daniel 9:16-19).

God heard and signally answered this earnest, heart-felt petition, for we read: "And while I was speaking, and praying, and confessing my sin and the sin of my people Israel, and presenting my supplication before the Lord my God for the holy mountain of my God; Yea, while I was speaking in prayer, even the man Gabriel, whom I have seen in the vision at the beginning, being caused to fly swiftly, touched me about the time of the evening oblation. And he informed me, and talked with me, and said, O, Daniel, I am now come forth to give thee skill and understanding. At the beginning of thy supplications the commandment came forth, and I am come to show thee; for thou art greatly beloved: therefore understand the matter, and consider the vision" (Daniel 9:20-23).

The exact year of Messiah's coming was then predicted. "Seventy weeks are determined upon thy people and upon thy holy city, to finish the transgression, and to make an end of sins, and make reconciliation for inquiry, and to bring in everlasting righteousness, and to seal up the vision and prophecy, and to anoint the most Holy. Know therefore and understand, that from the going forth of the commandment to restore and to build Jerusalem unto the Messiah the Prince shall be seven weeks, and threescore and two weeks: the street shall be built again, and the wall, even in troublous times. And after threescore and two weeks shall Messiah be cut off, but not for himself: and the people of the prince that shall come shall destroy the city [Jerusalem] and the sanctuary; and the end thereof shall be with a flood, and unto the end of the war desolations are determined. And he shall confirm the covenant with many for one week: and in the midst of the week he shall cause the sacrifice and the oblation to cease" (Daniel 9:24-27).

This forecast, so sublime in its conception, and so far-reaching in its implication, is not too difficult to grasp. The heavenly messenger informed Daniel that his prayer in behalf of the Hebrew nation had been heard, and that he had come to inform the petitioner as to what the future held in store for his earthly people. The angel then informed him, that a period of seventy weeks was allotted to the Jews. This period was to begin at the time that the commandment went forth to restore and to build Jerusalem. From that time, until the coming of Messiah the Prince, was to be seven weeks, plus sixty-two weeks, or a total of sixty-nine weeks.

The seventy-week period which was allotted to the Hebrews counting seven days to the week, equals 490 days. Inasmuch as this is a prophecy, these days are prophetic and not literal days. It is a well-established Bible rule that a day in prophecy stands for a year. (See Numbers 14:34 and also Ezekiel 4:6.) In other words, God in His infinite love and mercy granted the Hebrew nation an extension, an additional probationary time of 490 literal years, in which to redeem in a measure their errors of the past.

In order accurately to trace the time covered by this prophecy, and to establish with certainty its fulfillment, it is of paramount importance for us to know when this period of 490 years began. The above prophecy states that the 490-year period was to begin with the issuing of the decree "to restore and to build Jerusalem." If we, therefore, can find out in what year that decree went forth, we will be able to tell with absolute certainty when the 490-year period ended. Was such a decree issued? If so, when and by whom?

The Bible furnishes us this important information in the sixth chapter of the book of Ezra, verse 14. We read: "And the elders of the Jews builded, and they prospered through the prophesying of Haggai the prophet and Zechariah the son of Iddo. And they builded, and finished it, according to the commandment of the God of Israel, and according to the commandment of Cyrus, and Darius, and Artaxerxes king of Persia."

From the foregoing it is clear that not one king merely, but three kings—Cyrus, Darius, and Artaxerxes—issued a decree, or commandment, of restoration. Which of these three decrees constitutes the starting point of this great prophetic period? Or, in other words, which of these decrees gave the Hebrews absolute and complete authority "to restore and to build Jerusalem"? It is very evident that the decrees of Cyrus and Darius were not sufficient to complete the work of restoration, since it was necessary for Artaxerxes to issue the final, supplementary decree.

These three kings, in originating, reaffirming, and completing the decree, brought it to the perfection required by the prophecy. In the third decree ample authorization was given the children of Israel not only to restore and to rebuild Jerusalem, but also to establish their system of worship, giving them every facility and incentive to carry out in every detail the instruction that God had given them. This decree of Artaxerxes was issued in the year 457 B.C., and is recorded in the book of Ezra as follows: "Artaxerxes, king of kings, unto Ezra the priest....I make a decree, that all they of the people of Israel, and of his priests and Levites, in my realm, which are minded of their own freewill to go up to Jerusalem, go with thee" (Ezra 7:12, 13). (See also verses 14-26.)

The accuracy of the date of this decree—457 B.C.—is confirmed by an unimpeachable witness, the Bible. The Scripture declares that this decree was issued by Artaxerxes in the seventh year of his reign. (See Ezra 7:7.) Sir Isaac Newton, the renowned scientist, mathematician, and astronomer, aided by Ptolemy's celebrated "Cannon," (which lists the dates on which the kings of that period began to reign, and synchronizes those dates with the solar eclipses which occurred at that time), proved beyond the shadow of a doubt that the date of Artaxerxes' accession to the throne was 464 B.C. The seventh year of his reign was, therefore, 457 B.C. In that year he issued the historic decree, which went into effect in the fall of the same year.

Thus we find that the year when King Artaxerxes issued his famous decree was 457 B.C. With 457 B.C. as our starting point from which to reckon the 490-year period, we have the key to this most important and momentous prophecy.

The angel Gabriel announced to Daniel the prophet, "that from the going forth of the commandment to restore and to build Jerusalem" (which as stated, went into effect in the fall of 457 B.C.), unto the appearing of the Messiah, would be sixty-nine prophetic weeks. Sixty nine weeks equal 483 days. Since, according to scriptural interpretation, a prophetic day equals a year, these are 483 literal years. From 457 B.C., which is our starting point, we must add 483 years to take us to the long-looked-for Messiah of the Hebrews. The word "Messiah" means "the Anointed one." Counting 483 years from the autumn of 457 B.C., brings us to the autumn of A.D. 27, *the year when the Messiah, the Anointed One, was to appear.* By limiting the advent of the Messiah to a definite and specific time, this prophecy constitutes the key-stone of all the Messianic prediction of Scripture.

Did anyone appear in A.D. 27 who fulfilled all the Messianic specifications of Holy decree and who was anointed as the Messiah, as was predicted in the above prophecy of Daniel? History and chronology agree with the Bible, and all with one accord testify that Jesus was anointed as the Messiah in the fall of A.D. 27. We quote: "Now in the fifteenth year of the reign of Tiberius Caesar, Pontius Pilate being governor of Judea, and Herod being tetrarch of Galilee, and his brother Phillip tetrarch of Iturea and of the region of Trachonitis, and Lysanius the tetrarch of Abilene, Annas and Caiaphas being the high priests, the word of God came unto John the son of Zacharias in the wilderness" (Luke 3:1, 2).

Here are historically authenticated names of rulers who exercised authority in their respective realms at the time that John, the forerunner of the Redeemer (see prophecy concerning John in Isaiah 40:1-3), publicly announced the Messiah's appearance. Chronologically, the fifteenth year of the reign of Tiberius Caesar coincided with the year A.D. 27! John, who was born about six months before the Messiah (see Luke 1:11-17, 26-31, 36), began his labors at the close of A.D. 26. In the autumn of A.D. 27, Jesus was anointed immediately following His baptism by John. We quote: "It came to pass, that Jesus also being baptized, and praying, the heaven was opened, And the Holy Ghost descended in a bodily shape like a dove upon him, and a voice came from heaven, which said, Thou art my beloved Son; in thee I am well pleased" (Luke 3:21, 22).

"God anointed Jesus of Nazareth with the Holy Spirit and with power: who went about doing good, and healing all that were oppressed of the devil; for God was with him" (Acts 10:38).

This anointing of Jesus with the Holy Spirit at His baptism occurred in A.D. 27. After His divine anointing: "Jesus came into Galilee, preaching the gospel [or good news] of the kingdom of God, And saying, *The time is fulfilled,* and the kingdom of God is at hand: repent ye, and believe the gospel" (Mark 1:14, 15).

What did Jesus mean by the words, *"the time is fulfilled"*? He simply announced to the world that the 483-year prophecy had ended, and that He, the Messiah, had come in exact fulfillment of the angel Gabriel's time prophecy. In Jesus alone every feature of the time prophecy meets its literal and accurate fulfillment.

The Talmud admits that the Messiah was due to appear about two thousand years ago. In Tract Sanhedrin, Folio 97, column 1, is found the following statement: "The tradition of the school of Elijah. The world is to stand 6,000 years; 2,000 confusion; 2,000 the law; 2,000 the days of the Messiah."

Rashi, the eminent Hebrew commentator, referring to this quotation from the Talmud, says: "After the 2,000 years of the Law, according to the decree, Messiah ought to have come, and the wicked kingdom should have been destroyed, and Israel's state of servitude should have ended."

*   *   *

The time of the Messiah's Death was predicted in the Bible. The Messiah did appear at the end of sixty-nine prophetic weeks. Since, however, God allotted seventy to be fulfilled the angel Gabriel declared (see Daniel 9:26), that the Messiah was to be "cut off," or put to death, "but not for himself." His death was to be substitutionary. "In the midst of the week he shall cause the *sacrifice and the oblation to cease*" (Verse 27). In other words, His death was to put an end to the sacrificial system which foreshadowed His supreme sacrifice for the sins of the world. When He, the antitype, fulfilled the work which all these sacrifices merely typified, there was no further need for the shedding of any more sacrificial blood, inasmuch as He had paid the supreme redemption price with His own precious blood.

The exact year of the Messiah's death was also foretold by the angel in the following words: "He [the Messiah] shall confirm the covenant with many for one week; and in the *midst of the week* he shall cause the sacrifice and the oblation to cease" (Daniel 9:27).

A prophetic week, as we already know, equals seven literal years. The "midst" of seven is three and one half. The Messiah was to cause the sacrifices to cease three and one half years after His anointing. A study of the New Testament reveals the fact that Jesus ministered to the people exactly three and one half years—from the time of His anointing in October, A.D. 27, to the time of His death in April, A.D. 31. He was crucified in the spring, at the time of the Passover Feast. He died at the ninth hour, which was three o'clock in the afternoon, at the exact hour when the paschal lamb was to be slain,—namely,—"between the two evenings" (Exodus 12:6).

According to the Jewish reckoning of time, twelve, noon was called the evening of the day, and six o'clock in the evening was called the evening of the night. "Between the two evenings," would, therefore be three o'clock in the afternoon, which was the very hour when Jesus died. Of Him the colorful prophet Isaiah wrote: "He was wounded for our transgressions, he was bruised for our iniquities: the chastisement of our peace was upon him; and with his stripes we are healed. All we like sheep have gone astray; we have turned every one to his own way; and the Lord hath laid on him the iniquity of us all. He was oppressed, and he was afflicted, yet he opened not his mouth: he is brought as a lamb to the slaughter, and as sheep before her shearers is dumb, so he openeth not his mouth" (Isaiah 53:5-7).

When the loud cry, "It is finished," came from the lips of the Messiah, the priests were officiating in the temple. It was the hour of the evening sacrifice. The lamb representing the Messiah had been brought to be slain. Clothed in his significant and beautiful dress, the priest stood with lifted knife, as did Abraham when he was about to slay his son. With intense interest the people were looking on. But the earth trembles and quakes; for the Lord Himself draws near. With a rending noise the inner veil of the temple is torn from top to bottom by an unseen hand, throwing open to the gaze of the multitude a place once filled with the presence of God....All is terror and confusion. The priest is about to slay the victim; but the knife drops from his nerveless hand, and the lamb escapes. (See Matthew 27:45-51.)

From that hour the animal sacrifices lost their meaning, for type had met Antitype. Jesus is indeed the true paschal "Lamb" to whom the whole divinely-ordained system of sacrifices pointed.

Also the destruction of Jerusalem was foretold in Scripture. The angel Gabriel predicted further that after the Messiah was "cut off," Jerusalem would be destroyed. We read: "The people of the prince that shall come shall destroy the city and the sanctuary" (Daniel 9:26).

At the time of the Messiah's death, there still remained three and one-half years of the 490 years which had been apportioned to the Jewish nation. The Messiah died in the spring of A.D. 31. For exactly three and one-half years after Jesus' death, His disciples labored untiringly in Judea. "confirming the covenant." These Hebrew apostles preached repentance and forgiveness of sin through the divine sacrifice of the blessed Saviour Jesus. In the year A.D. 34, Stephen, the first early church martyr of the Messiah, the "Anointed One," was slain in a wave of persecution, and from that time forth, the believers were scattered to the ends of the earth, and went everywhere proclaiming the good news of salvation to all peoples—to the Gentiles, as well as to the Hebrews.

Thus we see that the 490 years which were "cut off" or determined upon Daniel's people, terminated in the year A.D. 34. From the middle of 457 B.C., when the decree went into effect, to the middle of A.D. 34, is exactly 490 years.

Thirty-six years later, in the year A.D. 70, Jerusalem was conquered by the Romans under the command of the Roman general Titus. The temple was burned and the Hebrew people were dispersed. Every feature of the angel Gabriel's forecast was fulfilled at the appointed time. There can be no doubt, therefore, that according to the Scriptures Jesus is the true Saviour.

*   *   *

When Jesus hung upon the cross He prayed for His persecutors: "Father," He pleaded, "forgive them; for they know not what they do" (Luke 23:34). Although the Hebrews grievously sinned against their own blessed Messiah when they rejected Him, He still loved them, and supplicated our heavenly Father that they might be forgiven.

In the Day of Atonement prayerbook, section *Musaph le-Yom Kippur,* we read the following words:

"The Messiah, our righteousness, has turned away from us.... It was He who was wounded for our transgressions.... By His stripes we are healed....I, Eternal One, create Him again at the time that He should be created....Bring Him up from the circle [of the earth]....To proclaim unto us [the good news] in mount Lebanon for the second time, by the hand of *Yinnon* [the Messiah]."

This pathetically touching prayer, which quotes parts of the Messianic prophecy of Isaiah chapter 53, was evidently composed by one who believed that the Messiah had already come for the first time. Indeed, the Messiah appeared at the very time appointed for His coming. It is true that we are healed "by His stripes." It is also true that He is coming the second time, in the future to end the reign of sin with its sorrows and woes, and eventually to establish His kingdom of peace, justice, and righteousness. He did not fail to come the first time, nor will He fail to come the second time. Let all true worshippers prepare for that glorious event.

However, in order to be ready for the second coming of Jesus, we must avail ourselves of what the Messiah has done for us at His first coming. At His first Advent, the Messiah by His substitutionary death made salvation from sin a reality for every one who repents and accepts Him as his personal Redeemer and Saviour. At His second coming the Messiah will gather in the fruit of His amazing sacrifice, the trophies of His victory and grace.

Acknowledging that He suffered and died for you, that He loved you and voluntarily gave Himself for you, your heavenly Father will for Jesus' sake forgive your sins and give you a new heart and a new spirit, enabling you to be justified in His sight. And when the Messiah returns in power and glory, you will be among the redeemed who will say: "This is our God; we have waited for him, and he will save us: this is the Lord; we have waited for him, we will be glad and rejoice in his salvation" (Isaiah 25:9).

5

Jesus as the Saviour

JESUS AS THE SAVIOUR

In 1948 or 1949 the Associated Press reported a movement among Hebrew leaders in newly established Israel to give Jesus of Nazereth a new trial. The purpose of this trial was to determine whether or not the Sanhedrin two thousand years ago was justified in pronouncing the death sentence upon Him. It was hoped that an unprejudiced and exhaustive investigation of the Scriptures by competent Rabbis would determine and forever settle the question of whether Jesus of Nazareth was or was not the promised Saviour of the world.

We will not attempt to predict what the final results of such an investigation would have been. We believe, however, that the exhaustive search into, and thorough examination of the Scriptures would have proved most profitable.

Many learned people acknowledge the fact that Jesus was a great man. Rabbis eulogize Him as an outstanding teacher of truth. But all this can be said of other leaders as well. Confucious, Buddha, Socrates, Plato, Gandhi, are all regarded as great religious teachers and thinkers. But Jesus claimed to be the Saviour. The following is a part of an interview between Jesus and a Samaritan woman at Jacob's well: "The woman saith unto him, I know that the Messias [Saviour] cometh, which is called Christ: when he is come, he will tell us all things. Jesus saith unto her, I that speak unto thee am He" (John 4:25, 26).

The following is a conversation that took place between the Saviour and His disciples, and is recorded in Matthew 16:13-17: "When Jesus came into the coasts of Caesarea Philippi, he asked his disciples, saying, Whom do men say that I, the Son of man, am?

And they said, Some say that thou art John the Baptist; some, Elias; and others, Jeremias, or one of the prophets. He saith unto them, But whom say ye that I am? And Simon Peter answered and said, Thou art the Christ, the Son of the Living God. And Jesus answered and said unto him, Blessed art thou, Simon Barjona; for flesh and blood hath not revealed it unto thee, but my Father which is in heaven."

After His betrayal, Jesus was brought before the Sanhedrin, and Caiaphas, the unqualified high priest, in the presence of the Ecclesiastical Council, solemnly addressed Him in this manner: "...I adjure thee by the living God, that thou tell us whether thou be the Christ, the Son of God. Jesus saith unto him, *Thou hast said...*" (Matthew 26:63, 64).

From the foregoing Scriptures it is very clear that Jesus regarded Himself as the Saviour, and as such He accepted the homage of man. Jesus either was the Saviour, or He was not. To regard Him merely as a good man or a great teacher is not consistent, for a good man will not assume the title of divine Saviour unless he has an absolute right to it. It is one thing to acknowledge and accept His claim as the blessed Saviour. The world has had many great teachers; but according to the Scriptures there can be but one and only one true heaven-accepted Saviour. The true Saviour must appear at a definite time, and must accomplish a specific work. If Jesus does not fulfill all the predictions of Scripture, we cannot accept His claim; but if He meets all the specifications as outlined in Holy Writ, we must accept the facts and acknowledge the truth. There can be no compromise and no neutrality on such a vital issue as this!

*   *   *

The God of all creation has given us a perfect standard by which we may test the claims of Jesus. This divine standard by which we may judge all Messianic claims is none other than the Old Testament. These Scriptures are the acid test of the genuineness or falsity of all the Messianic claims of Jesus. We read: "To the law and to the testimony: if they speak not according to this word, it is because there is no light in them" (Isaiah 8:20).

As we study the New Testament record, we discover that Jesus was supported by Old Testament Scriptures in all that He said and did. All His claims to Messiahship were based upon the writings of the earlier prophets.

Six hundred years before the Saviour was born, one of the holy prophets predicted that Israel's Deliverer was to be born in the city of Bethlehem. We quote: "But thou, Bethlehem Ephratah, though thou be little among the thousands of Judah, yet out of thee shall He come forth unto me that is to be ruler in Israel; whose goings forth have been from of old, from everlasting" (Micah 5:2).

It should be noted that this "ruler" who was to be born in Bethlehem, has existed from the days of eternity, from "everlasting." He is the divine Messiah.

The fulfillment of this prophecy is recorded in Matthew 2:1-6: "Now when Jesus was born in Bethlehem of Judea in the days of Herod the king, behold, there came wise men from the east to Jerusalem, saying, Where is he that is born King of the Jews? for we have seen his star in the east, and are come to worship him. When Herod the king had heard these things, he was troubled, and all Jerusalem with him. And when he had gathered all the chief priests and scribes of the people together, he demanded of them where the Christ should be born. And they said unto him, In Bethlehem of Judea: for thus it is written by the prophet, And thou Bethlehem, in the land of Juda, art not the least among the princes of Juda; for out of thee shall come a Governor, that shall rule my people Israel."

The joy of heralding the birth of the Saviour should have been shared by the leaders of Israel, but, the Scripture says, they knew not the time of their visitation; that is, they did not have a correct understanding of the Messianic predictions. God, therefore, revealed this great and most important event to the humble shepherds who were keeping watch by night on the hills of Bethlehem. The subject of the Saviour's coming was uppermost in their minds. They probably talked and prayed at length about the coming of this promised Deliverer who was to reign as King on the throne of David.

"And, lo, the angel of the Lord came upon them, and the glory of the Lord shone round about them; and they were sore afraid. And the angel said unto them, Fear not: for, behold, I bring you good tidings of great joy, which shall be to all people. For unto you is born this day in the city of David [which is Bethlehem] a Saviour, which is Christ the Lord. And this shall be a sign unto you; Ye shall find the babe wrapped in swaddling clothes, lying in a manger. And suddenly there was with the angel a multitude of the heavenly host praising God, and saying, Glory to God in the highest, and on earth peace, good will toward men" (Luke 2:9-14).

More than nineteen hundred years have passed since the events recorded in these Scriptures took place, and yet to this very day not a dissenting voice has been raised to deny that Jesus was indeed born in Bethlehem, the city of Judea, as the prophet said.

In other places in this book you will find most interesting and important information concerning the life and work of Jesus in the light of Bible teachings.

Jesus well knew that all the circumstances leading up to His death were to be a direct fulfillment of Old Testament Messianic predictions, as may be seen from the following Scripture: "Then he [Jesus] took unto him the twelve, and said unto them, Behold, we go up to Jerusalem, and all things that are written by the prophets concerning the Son of man shall be accomplished. For he shall be delivered unto the Gentiles, and shall be mocked, and spitefully entreated, and spitted on: And they shall scourge him, and put him to death: and the third day he shall rise again" (Luke 18:31-33).

"All things that are written by the prophets concerning the Son of Man shall be accomplished," Jesus declared. What a bold statement for the Saviour to make! He does not say, a few things, nor even, many things, but, all things must be fulfilled. What are these "all things" which were written by the prophets? They are the divinely inspired predictions that were recorded by the Old Testament seers concerning the Saviour's life and death.

The destiny of the world hangs upon the advent of the Saviour! He is the Redeemer of all the ages, the One who must redeem the human Adam's race, fallen because of sin. There must be no doubt as to His identity, and that is why God in His infinite love has given us such detailed predictions concerning both His life and His death.

*   *   *

God had revealed to the Hebrew prophets specific events that were to take place in connection with the Saviour's death and resurrection. There could not have been the slightest possible chance for all these forecasts to have been fulfilled in anyone else but the true Deliverer. There have been many false Messiahs, but not one of them ever claimed to be fulfilling the following Old Testament predictions. Jesus has been the only one to assert and maintain that every one of these forecasts pointed to Him, and were fulfilled in Him. We shall now consider twenty-five such predictions with their fulfillment in Jesus of Nazareth:

Sold for Thirty Pieces of Silver

This prophecy was made about the year 487 B.C.: "I said unto them, if ye think good, give me my price; and if not, forebear.

So they weighed for my price thirty pieces of silver" (Zechariah 11:12).

Fulfillment: "Then one of the twelve, called Judas Iscariot, went unto the chief priests, And said unto them, What will ye give me, and I will deliver him unto you? And they covenanted with him for thirty pieces of silver" (Matthew 26:14, 15).

Betrayed by a Friend

This prophecy was made about the year 1000 B.C.: "For it was not an enemy that reproached me; then I could have borne it: . . . But it was thou, a man mine equal, my guide, and mine acquaintance. We took sweet counsel together, and walked unto the house of God in company" (Psalm 55:12-14). (See also Psalm 41:9; Zechariah 13:6.)

Fulfillment: "Forthwith he [Judas] came to Jesus, and said, Hail, Master; and kissed him. And Jesus said unto him, Friend, wherefore art thou come? Then came they and laid hands on Jesus, and took him" (Matthew 26:49, 50). (See also Luke 22:47, 48.)

The Money Cast to the Potter in the House of the Lord

This prophecy was made about the year 487 B.C.: "And the Lord said unto me, Cast it unto the potter: a goodly price that I was prized at of them. And I took the thirty pieces of silver, *and cast them to the potter* in the house of the Lord" (Zechariah 11:13).

Fulfillment: "And he [Judas] cast down the pieces of silver *in the temple,* and departed, and went and hanged himself. And the chief priests took the silver pieces. . . . And they took counsel, and bought with them *the potter's field*" (Matthew 27:5-7). (See also verses 9, 10.)

The Disciples Forsook Him

This prophecy was made about the year 487 B.C.: ". . . smite the shepherd, and the sheep shall be scattered" (Zechariah 13:7).

Fulfillment: ". . . all the disciples forsook him, and fled" (Matthew 26:56). (See also Mark 14:27).

Accused by False Witnesses

This prophecy was made about the year 1000 B.C.: "False witnesses did rise up; they laid to my charge things that I knew not" (Psalms 35:11).

Fulfillment: "Now the chief priests, and elders, and all the council, sought false witness against Jesus, to put Him to death; . . . At the last came two false witnesses" (Matthew 26:59, 60).

Smitten and Spit Upon

This prophecy was made about 712 B.C.: "I gave my back to the smiters, and my cheeks to them that plucked off the hair; I hid not my face from shame and spitting" (Isaiah 50:6).

Fulfillment: "Then did they spit in his face, and buffeted him; and others smote him with the palms of their hands" (Matthew 26:67).

His Strength Failed Him

This prophecy was made about 1000 B.C.: "My knees are weak through fasting; and my flesh faileth of fatness" (Psalms 109:24).

Fulfillment: "And he bearing his cross went forth" (John 19:17). "...they laid hold upon one Simon,...and on him they laid the cross, that he might bear it after Jesus" (Luke 23:26).

Hands and Feet Pierced

This prophecy was made about 1000 B.C.: "For dogs have compassed me; the assembly of the wicked have inclosed me: they pierced my hands and my feet" (Psalms 22:16). (See also Zechariah 12:10).

Fulfillment: "And with him they crucify two thieves; the one on his right hand, and the other on his left. And the Scripture was fulfilled, which saith, And he was numbered with the transgressors" (Mark 15:27, 28).

Prayer for His Persecutors

This prophecy was made about 712 B.C.: He "...made intercession for the transgressors" (Isaiah 53:12).

Fulfillment: "Then said Jesus, Father, forgive them; for they know not what they do" (Luke 23:34).

People Shook Their Heads

This prophecy was made about 1000 B.C.: "I became also a reproach unto them: when they looked upon me they shook their heads" (Psalm 109:25).

Fulfillment: "And they that passed by reviled him, wagging their heads" (Matthew 27:39).

People Ridiculed Him

This prophecy was made about 1000 B.C.: "He trusted on the Lord that he would deliver him: let him deliver him, seeing he delighted in him" (Psalm 22:8).

Fulfillment: "Likewise also the chief priests mocking him, with the scribes and elders, said...He trusted in God; let him deliver him now, if he will have him" (Matthew 27:41-43).

People Were Astonished

This prophecy was made about 1000 B.C.: "...they look and stare upon me" (Psalm 22:17).

Fulfillment: "And the people stood beholding" (Luke 23:35).

Garments Parted and Lots Cast

This prophecy was made about 1000 B.C.: "They part my garments among them, and cast lots upon my vesture" (Psalm 22:18).

Fulfillment: "Then the soldiers when they had crucified Jesus, took his garments, and made four parts, to every soldier a part; and also his coat: now the coat was without seam, woven from the top throughout. They said therefore among themselves, Let us not rend it, but cast lots for it, whose it shall be: that the Scripture might be fulfilled, which saith, They parted my raiment among them, and for my vesture they did cast lots" (John 19:23, 24).

His Agonizing Cry

This prophecy was made about 1000 B.C.: "My God, my God, why hast thou forsaken me?" (Psalm 22:1).

Fulfillment: "...Jesus cried wth a loud voice, saying...My God, my God, why hast thou forsaken me?" (Matthew 27:46).

Gall and Vinegar Given Him

This prophecy was made about 1000 B.C.: "They gave me also gall for my meat; and in my thirst they gave me vinegar to drink" (Psalm 69:21).

Fulfillment: "After this, Jesus...saith, I thirst. Now there was set a vessel full of vinegar...and put it to his mouth" (John 19:28, 29). (See also Matthew 27:34.)

Committed Himself to God

This prophecy was made about 1000 B.C.: "Into thine hand I commit my spirit" (Psalm 31:5).

Fulfillment: "And when Jesus had cried with a loud voice, he said, Father, into thy hands I commend my spirit" (Luke 23:46).

Friends Stood Afar Off

This prophecy was made about 1000 B.C.: "My lovers and my friends stand aloof from my sore [stroke, margin,] and my kinsmen stand afar off" (Psalm 38:11).

Fulfillment: "And all his acquaintance, and the women that followed him from Galilee, stood afar off, beholding these things" (Luke 23:49).

His Bones Not Broken

This prophecy was made about 1000 B.C.: "He keepeth all his bones: not one of them was broken" (Psalm 34:20).

Fulfillment: "But when they came to Jesus and saw that he was dead already, they brake not his legs:...For these things were done, that the Scripture should be fulfilled, A bone of him shall not be broken" (John 19:33-36).

His Heart Was Broken

This prophecy was made about 1000 B.C.: "...My heart is like wax; it is melted in the midst of my bowels" (Psalm 22:14). "Reproach hath broken my heart" (Psalm 69:20).

Fulfillment: "But one of the soldiers with a spear pierced his side, and forthwith came there out blood and water" (John 19:34).

The blood and water running out of His pierced side indicated that His heart had literally burst. That this is in accord with physiology is confirmed by Drs. L. Lloyd Massey and Odis Kendrick, Jr.: "The heart is enclosed in a strong bag or sac, known as the pericardium. The inner surface of the pericardium and the outer surface of the heart are very smooth, and between them there is always a small amount of watery fluid, thus preventing friction.

"When dying is prolonged and accompanied by much suffering, this watery fluid might increase markedly, giving reality to the Bible statement that when the side of Jesus was pierced by the Roman spear, blood and water gushed forth. The pericardial space had been entered."

Another prominent physician states: "The cause now assigned for the death of Jesus, namely, the rupture of the heart from agony of mind, has been proved to be the result of an actual power in nature, fully adequate to the effect, really present without counteraction, minutely agreeing with all the facts of the case, and necessarily implied by them, this cause must, according to the principles of inductive reasoning, be regarded as demonstrated."

Darkness over the Land

This prophecy was made about 787 B.C.: "And it shall come to pass in that day, saith the Lord God, that I will cause the sun to go down at noon, and I will darken the earth in the clear day" (Amos 8:9).

Fulfillment: "Now from the sixth hour there was darkness over all the land unto the ninth hour" (Matthew 27:45).

The Jews divided the day from sunrise to sunset into twelve hours. This would make the sixth hour about noon, and the ninth hour three o'clock.

Buried in a Rich Man's Tomb

This prophecy was made about 712 B.C.: "And he made his grave with...the rich in his death" (Isaiah 53:9).

Fulfillment: "When the even was come, there came a rich man of Arimathea, named Joseph, who also himself was Jesus' disciple: He went to Pilate, and begged the body of Jesus....And when Joseph had taken the body, he wrapped it in a clean linen cloth, And laid it in his own new tomb" (Matthew 27:57-60).

Messiah to Rise from the Dead

This prophecy was made about 1000 B.C.: "For thou wilt not leave my soul in hell [sheol, or grave]; neither wilt thou suffer thine Holy One to see corruption" (Psalm 16:10).

Fulfillment: "He [David], seeing this before, spake of the resurrection of the Christ, that his soul was not left in hell [grave], neither his flesh did see corruption. This Jesus hath God raised up, whereof we are all witnesses" (Acts 2:31, 32).

After the resurrection of Jesus, two of His disciples were on their way to a town called Emmaus. They were discussing the strange events connected with the death and resurrection of the Messiah.

And "...Jesus himself drew near, and went with them. But their eyes were holden that they should not know him. And he said unto them, What manner of communications are these that ye have one to another, as ye walk, and are sad?

"And the one of them whose name was Cleopas, answering said unto him, Art thou only a stranger in Jerusalem, and hast not known the things which are come to pass there in these days? And he said unto them, What things? And they said unto him, Concerning Jesus of Nazareth, which was a prophet mighty in deed and word before God and all the people: And how the chief priests and our rulers delivered him to be condemned to death, and have crucified him....And beside all this, today is the third day since these things were done....Then he [Jesus] said unto them, O fools, and slow of heart to believe *all* that the prophets have spoken: Ought not the Christ to have suffered these things, and to enter into his glory? And beginning at Moses and all the prophets he expounded unto them in all the Scriptures the things concerning himself" (Luke 24:15-27).

Thus the combined testimony of all the Hebrew prophets points to Jesus, of Nazareth, as the true Messiah. No longer is He in Joseph's new tomb, for He rose and, as a living Saviour, "ever liveth to make intercession" for us. Never need we feel desolate or forsaken, if we but believe Him to be our Saviour, who represents us before the throne of the eternal God.

* * *

For many centuries, Jesus the Saviour has been separated from us. What ecstasy, what surpassing joy fills the heart and mind of anyone who upon examining the Scriptures relating to the Messiah, discovers in them the evidence that this lowly, unobtrusive Nazarene, this heretofore stranger, is indeed and in truth his own, his very own flesh and blood, his Saviour and King! Indeed, all the intelligences of the heavenly host rejoice with him as they witness the happy re-union!

God implores us to study and examine the prophecies, for they "are written, that ye might believe that Jesus is the Christ...and that believing ye might have life through his name" (John 20:31).

6

Jesus as the High Priest

JESUS AS THE HIGH PRIEST

In these momentous and soul-searching times, when harsh and oftentimes unrealistic decisions confront all governments and nations, a retrospective view of Israel's sacred, but sometimes marred, history should prove most profitable to students of Biblical history. We are informed in the Scriptures that Israel's experiences in the past "happened unto them for ensamples [object lessons]: and they are written for our admonition, upon whom the ends of the world are come" (I Cor. 10:11). A thoughtful contemplation of Israel's past history would enable us better to chart not only our present, but our future course as well; and would materially aid us in our struggle to reach the desired haven of rest, peace and security. This thought is beautifully expressed by the Hebrew prophet, who said: "Thus saith the Lord, Stand ye in the ways, and see, and ask for the *old paths,* where is the good way, and walk therein, and *ye shall find rest* for your souls" (Jeremiah 6:16).

*   *   *

A wealth of information and many vital and needful lessons and statistics may be gleaned from the study of the ancient Hebrew temple services. These rituals embodied truths of profound spiritual significance. It was God's plan and design that these truths be taught to the surrounding nations who were ignorant of Him and of the plan of salvation. To this end God chose Israel to be His special and peculiar people. They were to be the spiritual teachers and guides to the heathen peoples around them. Their mission was to explain the meaning of the sanctuary services, and to teach the great truths of redemption which these services typified.

They were to prepare the way for the soon coming Saviour—not to supplant the need for his coming!

In entrusting this exalted mission to Israel, God had declared, "Ye shall be unto me a kingdom of priests, and an holy nation" (Exodus 19:6). The Levites were to act as go-betweens, or mediators, between God and the people. Why was this special work of mediation necessary, you ask? It was for the same reason that attorneys, barristers, and advocates are necessary in our present civilization. We all agree that it is important to have men who are thoroughly versed in the law to mediate between the accused—the one who has broken the law—and the judge, before whom the lawbreaker is arraigned. Mankind has transgressed God's holy laws. This has caused a separation and an impassable barrier between man and his Maker. We read: "Behold, the Lord's hand is not shortened that it cannot save; neither his ear heavy, that it cannot hear: But your iniquities have separated between you and your God, and your sins have hid his face from you, that he will not hear" (Isaiah 59:1, 2).

From the Scripture it is evident that man needs an advocate with the Father. Man is, therefore, in dire need of an intercessor, a sympathetic liaison or connecting link, between himself and God. Israel's priesthood, and the ritual services they performed, were designed to direct the mind of the beholder to the true mediatorial system which God had instituted for reconciling man to Himself. In other words, the ministry of the Levite priests in the earthly sanctuary served as a type, a miniature representation, of the true and real mediatorial work which is theologically going on in Heaven in behalf of repentant sinners. It was a practical illustration designed to teach the most important truth, namely, that through the mediation of an Intercessor, man can once more enjoy the communion with God which he has forfeited because of sin.

*   *   *

In Abraham's day the priesthood was bestowed upon the first-born son. This custom was observed in Israel till shortly after Israel's deliverance from Egyptian bondage. (See Exodus 13:1, 2, and Exodus 22:29.) Subsequently, however, the Lord chose the tribe of Levi for the special service of the sanctuary. It is written of them: "And the Lord spake unto Moses, saying, and I behold, I have taken the Levites from among the children of Israel instead of all the first born that openeth the matrix among the children of Israel: therefore the Levites shall be mine;

"Because all the firstborn are mine; for on the day that I smote all the firstborn in the land of Egypt I hallowed unto me all the firstborn of Israel, both man and beast: mine shall they be: I am the Lord" (Numbers 3:11-13).

Nevertheless a redemption price was still required of the people for their firstborn.

While the entire tribe of Levi was chosen for the work of the sanctuary, the work of mediating between God and His people was laid wholly upon Aaron and his sons (see Numbers 18:1-6), and it was expressly forbidden for any other Levite to assume the functions of a priest. It is likewise true that when Korah, Dathan, and Abiram presumptuously coveted the priesthood by burning incense in defiance of God's express commands, they were guilty of high treason against the Lord. The Bible leads us to interpret that they were probably drunken during this tragic experience. Their wilful sin called down upon them and their families the judgments of God in swift retribution. The earth opened her mouth and swallowed them up with all that appertained to them. (See Numbers 16:8-33.)

* * *

The work of the priesthood was a most solemn one. The very dress of the priests betokened the sacred character of their work. Leviticus informs us that specific and detailed instruction was given by God concerning the priestly attire. "And thou shalt make holy garments for Aaron thy brother for glory and for beauty" (Exodus 28:2). A well-known Baptist clergyman and church administrator, Dr. Harold G. Sanders, gives us a beautiful description of the priest's dress as it is depicted in Scripture:

"The robe of the common priest was of white linen, and woven in one piece. It extended nearly to the feet, and was confined about the waist by a white linen girdle embroidered in blue, purple, and red. A linen turban, or miter, completed his outer costume." Moses at the burning bush was directed to put off his sandals, for the ground whereon he stood was holy. So the priests were not to enter the sanctuary with shoes on their feet. Particles of dust cleaving to them would desecrate the holy place. They were to leave their shoes in the court before entering the temple sanctuary, and also to wash both their hands and their feet before ministering in the tabernacle or at the altar of burnt-offering. Such a statute was constantly taught as a lesson that all defilement must be put away from those who would approach into the presence of God.

The garments of the high priest were of costly material and beautiful workmanship, befitting his exalted station. In addition to the linen dress of the common priest, he wore a robe of blue, also woven in one piece. Around the skirt it was ornamented with golden bells and pomegranates of blue, purple, and scarlet. Outside of this was the ephod, a shorter garment of gold, blue, purple, scarlet, and white. It was confined by a girdle of the same colors, beautifully wrought. The ephod was sleeveless, and on its gold-embroidered shoulder pieces were set two onyx stones, bearing the names of the twelve tribes of Israel.

Everything connected with the apparel and deportment of the priests was to be such as to impress the beholder with a sense of the holiness of God, the sacredness of His worship, and the purity required of those who came into His presence.

*   *   *

At the inauguration of the tabernacle service an elaborate and sacred ceremony took place. Both the sanctuary and the priests were anointed with holy oil, and the blood of a sacrifice was sprinkled upon Aaron and his sons, typifying the merits of the shed blood of the Messiah, which alone qualified them to fill acceptably their holy office as priests.

The yearly round of services consisted of two divisions. Every day of the year (excepting on the Day of Atonement), the priests officiated only in the first apartment of the sanctuary, which was called the Holy place. Day in and day out every penitent sinner brought his sacrifice to the door of the tabernacle and placing his hand upon the head of the animal confessed his sin, thus in figure transferring his sin from himself to the innocent victim. Then the penitent slew the animal and the blood was taken by the priest into the first apartment of the sanctuary, and sprinkled upon the veil that separated the first apartment from the second. This blood of the *paroches*—the veil, represented the sins of the penitent. These sins defiled the sanctuary, and it was not until the Day of Atonement, when the accumulated sins of the people were covered, that the sanctuary was cleansed of this defilement. This work of cleansing was done by the High Priest.

We have already learned that this annual round of services in the Priestly sanctuary served "unto the example and shadow of heavenly things" (Hebrews 8:5).

*   *   *

In the struggle between good and evil no mere human help will avail us. Divine power from the Holy Spirit alone can give us the victory over the powers of darkness and sin. This superhuman help is within our reach in the person of the Saviour. In another chapter abundant scriptural evidence is presented that Jesus is indeed the Messiah and our divine Mediator. However, in order that He might become our merciful and faithful High Priest and Mediator, it was necessary for Him to come to this earth in the form of man, for only a divine-human Mediator can unite man to God and thereby effect a reconciliation between the two. "Neither is there salvation in any other: for there is none other name under Heaven given among men, whereby we must be saved" (Acts 4:12).

This incarnation of the Son of God was foretold by Isaiah the prophet who predicted the Saviour would be born miraculously—of a virgin—and that His name would be Immanuel, which interpreted is, "God with us" (Isaiah 7:14). This prophecy was fulfilled when Jesus was born of the devout Hebrew maiden, the virgin, Mary. (See Matthew 1:18-23.)

Why this incarnation was necessary is explained in the following Scripture: "Wherefore in all things it behooved him to be made like unto his brethren, that he might be a merciful and faithful high priest in things pertaining to God, to make reconciliation for the sins of the people. For in that he himself hath suffered being tempted, he is able to succour them that are tempted" (Hebrews 2:17, 18).

The sufferings of the Saviour, and His substitutionary death for the sins of the world, are foretold in Isaiah 53. This prophecy was literally fulfilled when the Lord "laid on him [on Jesus the Saviour] the inquity of us all." He died on Calvary's tree a willing sacrifice for the sins of the world.

His resurrection was predicted by David, the sweet singer of Israel, who writes in Psalm 16:10 that God would not suffer his "Holy One to see corruption." Jesus, the Holy One, rose from the tomb before corruption had set in, a conqueror over death and the grave. (See Matthew 28:1-6.)

The Saviour's ascension to heaven was also foretold by David, and is recorded in Psalm 24:7-10. His mediatorial work in the heavenly sanctuary is described as follows: "The Lord [Jehovah] said unto my Lord [Adoni], sit thou at my right hand, until I make thine enemies thy footstool.... The Lord hath sworn, and will not repent, Thou art a priest *forever* after the order of Melchizedek" (Psalm 110:1, 4).

In this Scripture are represented two persons of the trinity—"Jehovah" and "Adoni." Jehovah, who is God the Father, is addressing Adoni—God the Son. The Father invites the Son to sit at His right hand, which is the position of great honor and distinction. In the same Scripture He designates the Son to be of the priestly order of Melchizedek, which signified an everlasting priesthood "a priest *forever.*"

The Melchizedek priesthood was superior to the Levitical. Concerning Melchizedek we read: "And Melchizedek *king* of Salem brought forth bread and wine: and he was the *priest of the most high God.* And he blessed him, and said, Blessed be Abram of the most high God, possessor of heaven and earth: And blessed be the most high God, which hath delivered thine enemies into thy hand. And he gave him tithes of all" (Genesis 14:18-20).

You will observe that this Melchizedek was greater than the Patriarch Abraham, for he blessed Abraham and received his tithes (or tenths) from him. He was not only king of Salem, but was also *Cohen L-El Elyon,* "priest of the most high God." Being both king and priest, Melchizedek represented an order of priesthood which was far superior to the Levitical priesthood, for under the Jewish theocracy no person could be both priest and king at the same time.

This Melchizedek, who was king and priest of the most high God, was a fitting type of Jesus our precious Saviour, who, the Scripture says, was "made a high priest for ever after the order of Melchizedek" (Hebrews 6:20). Thus our blessed Saviour is honored by the Father as both *king* and *priest.* In the following Scriptures the prophet Zechariah teaches this same truth concerning the exaltation of the Saviour:

". . . . Thus speaketh the Lord of hosts, saying, Behold, the *man* whose name is The Branch; and he shall grow up out of His place, and he shall build the *temple of the Lord.* Even he shall build the temple of the Lord; and he shall bear the glory, and shall *sit and rule upon his throne;* and he shall be a *priest* upon his throne and the council of peace shall be between them both" (Zechariah 6:12, 13).

The temple spoken of here is the heavenly temple, for it is not to be built by human hands, but by the Branch. Jeremiah the prophet, speaking of this Branch, writes as follows: "Behold, the days come, saith the Lord, that I will raise unto David a righteous Branch, and a King shall reign and prosper, and shall execute judgment and justice in the earth. In his days Judah shall be saved, and Israel shall dwell safely: this is his name whereby he shall be called, THE LORD OUR RIGHTEOUSNESS" (Jeremiah 23:5, 6).

This text informs us that the Man whose name is the *Branch,* who sprang from David, in whose days "Judah shall be saved," would be called "the Lord our righteousness." That is to say, He was to be both human and divine. The prophet Zechariah further informs us in the former text that this Branch is to be a *Priest*—a *Cohen*—and that the counsel between Him and the Father would be one of the peace for the human race.

All these predictions are significantly fulfilled in but one Being, and that One is Jesus.

*   *   *

The ascension of the Son of God is described in Acts 1:9-11. Following His ascension, His enthronement and inauguration as our high priest and mediator took place. This ceremony was performed on Pentecost, fifty days after His resurrection. (See Acts 2:30, 33; Philippians 2:9-11; Hebrews 2:9.)

The sum and substance of all that has thus far been presented is aptly stated by the apostle Paul: "We have such a high priest, who is set on the right hand of the throne of the majesty in the heavens; a minister of the sanctuary, and of the true tabernacle, which the Lord pitched, and not man" (Hebrews 8:1, 2).

What a never-failing source of comfort and hope it is to know that we have a divine-human Mediator, a Saviour at the throne of God, One who has experienced the disappointments, the sorrows, and the griefs which are the lot of humanity!

During a lull on the western front in World War II, General Hodges was called to Washington to attend an important conference with General George Marshall. In his absence, the enemy launched a powerful surprise attack against his army. His soldiers soon found themselves completely encircled by the attacking Germans and were facing total annihilation.

When the news concerning his army's impassé was flashed to the general at Washington, he asked permission to return immediately to his beleaguered men. He was advised against presumptuously exposing himself to danger, but to no avail. His thought was not for his personal safety. There was much more at stake! He thought of his gallant soldiers who were surrounded by the enemy's ring of steel. Commandeering a fast plane and defying the deadly barrage of gunfire, he rejoined his heroic, battle-scarred, and war-weary soldiers. Inspired by the presence of their fearless and beloved commander, his army fought valiantly until they made a breach in the enemy's formidable iron wall. Thus the historic "Battle of the Bulge," was won.

Looking down from heaven, the Captain of the Lord's hosts, the Son of God beheld us, His embattled children, besieged by Satan and his wicked host. He might have chosen to remain in the peaceful atmosphere of His heavenly home, but He did not do this. His heart of infinite love yearned after His earth-born children who were in such great peril. And so He came to cast in His lot with us.

He knew whither His steps were leading Him; He knew that He would be the target of the determined and relentless attacks of Satan. He was aware of the blood-stained path that lay before Him which would end in His agonizing death on the cross. But no considerations of personal safety could deter Him. He had counted the cost of man's redemption, and was willing to pay the staggering price with His own blood. And so,

> Out of the ivory palaces into a world of woe,
> Only His great eternal love made the Saviour go.

Although the lot He had chosen was the thorniest ever experienced by any earth being, the Son of God never faltered nor wavered till He had drunk the cup to its bitter dregs. He did not turn back until He had made the supreme sacrifice. In doing this He broke the power of the enemy, and triumphed over death and the grave. Having paid the price for our eternal redemption, He now, as our merciful and faithful High Priest Mediator, Lord and King, stands before His Father pleading the infinite merits of His supreme sacrifice in our behalf.

*   *   *

In view of this sacrifice which the Father and the Son were willing to make for our redemption, can we ever again feel desolate and forsaken, friendless and alone in this world? Do you think that God is indifferent to our needs, that He has forgotten us? He asks: "Can a woman forget her sucking child, that she should not have compassion on the son of her womb? Yea, they may forget, yet will I not forget thee. Behold, I have graven thee upon the *palms of my hands*" (Isaiah 49:15, 16). Those prints of the nails in the hands of our High Priest which He received when He was nailed to the cross, are a most eloquent assurance that heaven considers no sacrifice too great to pay in order to purchase our eternal salvation.

Our Saviour is on the eternal throne of God. He looks upon every soul that turns to Him as personal Saviour. He knows by experience what are the weaknesses of humanity, what are our wants and what are our temptations; for He was in all points tempted as we are, yet without sin. He is watching over you, trembling child of earth. Are you tempted? He will deliver. Are you weak? He will strengthen. Are you ignorant? He will enlighten. Are you wounded? He will heal. "He healeth the broken in heart, and bindeth up their wounds." "Come unto me," is His invitation. Whatever your anxieties and trials, spread out your case before the Lord. Your spirit will be braced for endurance. The way will be opened for you to disentangle yourself from embarrassment and difficulty. The weaker and more helpless you know yourself to be, the stronger will you become in His strength. The heavier your burdens, the more blessed the rest in casting them upon the Sin Bearer.

And so, let America thank God for the "anchor of the soul, both sure and steadfast, and which entereth into that within the veil [of the heavenly Holy of Holies]; Whither the forerunner is for us entered, even Jesus, made a High Priest forever after the order of Melchizedek" (Hebrews 6:19, 20).

"Wherefore he is able also to save them to the uttermost that come unto God by him, seeing he ever liveth to make intercession for them" (Hebrews 7:25).

Who can resist the Father's love and the tender, heaven-born appeals of the Son of God to yield Him our heart's deepest gratitude and affection? He is pleading with the lost multitudes. Will we not make this compassionate Jesus, our Saviour and Redeemer known throughout our beloved country and world?

7

The Existence of Angels

THE EXISTENCE OF ANGELS

Angels are mentioned in the Old Testament 109 times. Many people have the erroneous impression that the angels are the spirits of the righteous dead, but this is not true. The Bible plainly teaches that the angels were in existence before this world was created, or before the first person died. Many a mother has sung baby to sleep with this rhyme or lullaby,

> Hush, hush, little baby, don't you cry,
> You will be an angel by and by.

This lullaby simply is not true, because it has no proof in the Bible! Nowhere in the Bible does it say that we become angels when we die. According to the Bible, angels were in existence *before* the creation of this world. We read in Job 38:4, 7: "Where wast thou when I laid the foundations of the earth? declare, if thou hast understanding. . . . When the morning stars sang together, and all the sons of God shouted for joy?"

Here we find that the morning stars, a certain order of angels, sang together for joy at the time of creation.

We also find the angels were in existence before Abel, the first man to die. We read in Genesis 3:22-24: "And the Lord God said, Behold, the man is become as one of us, to know good and evil: and now, lest he put forth his hand, and take also of the tree of life, and eat, and live for ever: Therefore the Lord God sent him forth from the garden of Eden, to till the ground from whence he was taken. So he drove out the man; and he placed at the east of the garden of Eden cherubim, and a flaming sword which turned every way, to keep the way of the tree of life."

Here we find cherubim, an high order of angels, placed at the entrance of the garden of Eden to keep man out of it. Thus we read of angels before the first man, Abel, died. Therefore, we must concede that angels are not the spirits of the departed dead, because there were angels *before* sin ever entered the universe. Angels, according to the Holy Scriptures, are beings that were created by God in a higher form of life than man. Thus we read in Psalm 8:4, 5: "What is man, that thou art mindful of him? and the son of man, that thou visitest him? For thou hast made him a little lower than the angels, and hast crowned him with glory and honor."

Multitudes may ask the question, if there are real angels, why can not we see them? This question is easily answered through a simple illustration of the television. In every part of the world, in every home, in every room, no matter where you go, there is music, real life pictures, and voices, but we cannot hear or see them unless we use the appliance, which is more sensitive than our ears. Because of sin our hearing is not perfect. Before sin entered the world, man had perfect sight and perfect hearing, and if he had never sinned he would have remained that way, and he would have lived for eternity without ever seeing death. But after sin entered the world the length of his life, his sight, his hearing, and all of his senses were affected. The Bible says that man lived from eight to nine hundred years of age until the time of Noah's flood, which was many centuries after creation. But after the flood, his life became much shorter, and now we find the average man lives about sixty-eight years. Sin has marred the span of life to such an extent that not only the length of life is affected, but our senses as well. Thus we can understand why our hearing and our sight are affected. However, we do have the promise that when God shall create a new heaven and a new earth, that the righteous will be given perfect sight, hearing, and eternal life. As we cannot hear the music without the use of a physical organ, so it is that we cannot see the angels until God shall give us perfect sight; but if we are faithful some day we shall be able to see the angels and speak with them face to face. This is made plain in II Kings 6:15-17, where we find Elisha praying for the eyes of his servant so that he could see the multitude of angels that were there to help them. Notice this Biblical record:

"And when the servant of the man of God was risen early, and gone forth, behold, an host compassed the city both with horses and chariots. And his servant said unto him, Alas, my master! how shall we do? And he answered, Fear not: for they that be with us are more than they that be with them. And Elisha prayed, and said, Lord, I pray thee, open his eyes, that he may see. And the Lord opened the eyes of the young man; and he saw: and, behold, the mountain was full of horses and chariots of fire round about Elisha.

Elisha knew the angels were there, though man with mortal eyes could not see them. So he prayed that the Lord would open his servant's eyes, so that he could see the multitude of angels that were there to help them and protect them from the enemy.

*　　*　　*

It is a wonderful thought to know that there are angels standing by ready to help us every moment of the day. Only eternity in the realm made new will reveal the many times our guardian angel saved our lives.

In the Scriptures we learn that God has supernatural agencies to guide the steps of His earth-born children through the dangers and pitfalls of their life's journey. The Bible, as it were, lifts the veil which separates the visible from the invisible world and enables us to catch a glimpse of God's loving care and solicitude in behalf of His trusting and blood washed believing people. Exclaims the prophet: "The angel of the Lord encampeth round about them that fear Him, and delivereth them" (Psalm 34:7). Now, you can see that angels from the courts above attend the steps of every humble, trusting child of God.

We need only think of the forceful illustration of this truth in the life of Elisha the prophet just cited. When Elisha's servant saw the multitudes of angels encamped round about his master, his fear departed.

Could our eyes be opened, we, too, would be astonished and amazed at the constant activity and tender supplication of these heavenly messengers in our behalf as we, by our prayer, invited their protection.

*　　*　　*

Some may ask: Are these angels real beings, and do they possess real bodies? The prophet Isaiah describes angels in the following inspired language: "Each one had six wings; with twain he covered his face, and with twain he covered his feet, and with twain he did fly" (Isaiah 6:2).

Yet angels are called "spirits" in the Bible. In Psalm 104:4, we read that God "maketh Hs angels *spirits,* His ministers a flaming fire." How do we then explain that angels are described as possessing physical characteristics common to man at the same time that they are said to be "spirits." The explanation is twofold.

First of all, when Scripture speaks of physical characteristics of angels, these physical features are emblematic. Wings symbolize the ability and readiness of these beings to do the will of God as His messengers. The angel is said to cover his face and feet to show deep reverence in the presence of God.

Furthermore, God equips the angels with exactly those features and abilities essential to do His Divine bidding. Scripture clearly illustrates this. In the 18th chapter of Genesis we read that angels appeared in human form, and partook of Abraham's hospitality, eating the food prepared for them. In the 13th chapter of Judges it is recorded that an angel held converse with Manoah and his wife instructing them concerning their son Samson. In the 22nd chapter of Numbers, we read that an angel confronted Balaam in an effort to intercept his journey to the Moabites where he intended to curse Israel. Angels were seen by David, Lot, Gideon, Daniel, and many other Bible characters. Angels are God's messengers who do his pleasure "hearkening unto the voice of his word" (Psalm 103:20).

*   *   *

It is impossible for the human intellect to conceive of the power, glory, influence, and wisdom of these celestial beings. The Psalmist declares that they "excel in strength" (Psalm 103:20). These heavenly watchers shield the righteous from untold dangers, both seen and unseen. The Bible abounds with illustrations of the extra-ordinary interpositions of angels in man's behalf.

A typical example is found in Genesis 19. A wicked, lawless group of Sodomites inflamed by the vilest passions, gathered about Lot's house where two angels were being entertained for the night. As the angry multitude rushed in upon Lot in an attempt to break into his house, we are told: "They [the angels] smote the men that were at the door of the house with blindness, both small and great: so that they wearied themselves to find the door" (Genesis 19:11).

When the children of Israel were captives in Medo-Persia, Daniel the prophet, because of conspiracy against him, was cast into a den of fierce, voracious lions for praying to the God of heaven. Early the next morning, after passing a sleepless night, the king Darius hastened to the cave, and "cried with a lamentable voice...O

Daniel, servant of the living God, is thy God, whom thou servest continually, able to deliver thee from the lions?"

The prophet replied: "O king, live forever. My God hath sent his angel, and hath shut the lion's mouths, that they have not hurt me . . . . Then was the king exceeedingly glad for him, and commanded that they should take Daniel up out of the den. So Daniel was taken up out of the den, and no manner of hurt was found upon him, because he believed in his God" (Daniel 6:18-23).

Here again we see how the presence of one angel was sufficient to protect and deliver from physical harm and distress, one who suffered for righteousness' sake. Jehovah's vigilance and tender watchcare over His children is constant and untiring. Of them it is declared that "He that toucheth you toucheth the apple of His eye" (Zechariah 2:8). God permitted the enemies of Daniel to cast him into the lion's den, in order that He might make his deliverance more marked, and the defeat of his enemies more complete.

In the days of king Hezekiah, Jerusalem was besieged by a great throng of the Assyrian army. The proud and haughty Rabshakeh, one of Sennacherib's chief officers, insolently and blasphemously reviled the God of the Hebrews, and demanded the surrender of the city. He boasted that the gods of Assyria were superior in power to the God of Israel, and that his gods would deliver the Israelites into his hands. "For this cause Hezekiah the king, and the prophet Isaiah the son of Amoz, prayed and cried to heaven" (II Chronicles 32:20).

God answered the united prayers of His servants. He vindicated His name and made bare His mighty arm. We read: "And it came to pass that night, that the angel of the Lord went out, and smote in the camp of the Assyrians an hundred fourscore and five thousand" (II Kings 19:35). "All the mighty men of valour, and the leaders and captains in the camp of the king of Assyria" were slain (II Chronicles 32:21). Thus again we see how one angel brought to nought the boastful threats of the enemies of God, frustrating their plans for conquest and loot.

The Scriptures assure us that angels "encamp" round about them that "fear" God. (See Psalm 34:7.) It is most comforting and reassuring to know that those who love God and obey the Lord Jesus even though such fidelity and devotion means risking their lives, are the special object of God's protecting care. Angels from the realms of glory are commissioned to minister to these loyal servants of God, and to deliver them from bodily harm, if such a miracle is necessary in order to vindicate the Lord's honor.

This is strikingly illustrated by the experience of the three noble Hebrew young men during the Babylonian captivity. They were Hananiah, Mishael, and Azariah, whose names Nebuchadnezzar, king of Babylon, changed to Shadrach, Meshach, and Abednego.

This idolatrous monarch had set up a golden image on the plain of Dura, and decreed that all the government officials of his vast empire should attend the dedication of this image, and at a given signal, fall down and worship it. When the hour struck and the vast assembly fell down before the golden image, the Hebrew youths remained standing. They refused to render obeisance to the work of men's hands. The God of Abraham forbade the worship of idols, and they chose to obey the Commandments of the King of kings, though this conflicted with the decree of an earthly ruler.

When the haughty king of Babylon learned that these three youths had challenged his authority and had refused to worship his image, his fury and rage knew no bounds. He commanded that they appear before him without a moment's delay. Then, looking at them sternly, he asked them whether it was true that they refused to bow down and serve his gods, and warned them that unless they rendered homage to the golden image they would be cast into a "burning fiery furnace." Their intrepid reply was: "Our God whom we serve is able to deliver us from the burning fiery furnace, and he will deliver us out of thine hand, O king. But if not [that is, if God does not choose to deliver us], be it known unto thee, O king, that we will not serve thy gods, nor worship the golden image which thou hast set up." (See Daniel 3:1-18.)

"Full of fury," the king commanded that the three young men be cast into the furnace, and that its fires be intensified seven times for this occasion. Bound together, the three noble young men were thrown into the raging fiery furnace. The cruel, tyrannical ruler sat by and closely watched the proceedings, expecting to see the youths instantly scorched to death by the flames. But the God of Israel wrought a mightly miracle for these loyal, valiant young men. The fetters with which they were bound together, broke, and the three Hebrews walked around the fiery furnace unharmed and unscratched! The flames had no effect upon these youthful worshippers of God who feared the Majesty of heaven more than the wrath of an earthly monarch. And as king Nebuchadnezzar witnessed this amazing miracle, he trembled from head to foot, and commanded that the three heroes be lifted out of the furnace. Acknowledging the mighty power of the God of Abraham, Nebuchadnezzar exclaimed: "Blessed be the God of Shadrach, Meshach, and Abednego, who hath sent his angel, and delivered his servants that trusted in him, and have changed the king's word, and yielded their bodies, that they might not serve nor worship any god, except their own God" (Daniel 3:28).

The power and vigilance of the angels of Jehovah have not lessened with the passing of the centuries. Today, as of old, these celestial watchers stand ready to guide, protect, and deliver God's children who are obedient to the Holy Spirit even in the very face of death.

* * *

In Ezekiel 1:14 we read concerning the angels: "The living creatures ran and returned as the appearance of a flash of lightning." In this Scripture the prophet testifies that angels "run" with the speed of lightning. Science tells us that light travels at the enormous speed of 186,000 miles a second! It takes thousands and even millions of light years for a ray of light to reach our earth from very distant stars. Yet we learn from the following Scripture that it took an angel only a moment of time to span this huge distance. Said the angel Gabriel to the praying prophet Daniel: "At the beginning of thy supplications the commandment came forth, and I am come to shew thee; for thou are greatly beloved" (Daniel 9:23).

Heaven may seem far removed from our distraught and distressed world, yet in only a moment of time, indeed, at the very beginning of our supplication, the angel spans the vast abyss of space in order to bring comfort, protection, and deliverance. What an incentive to pray!

The eternal God has at His command an "innumerable company" of these shining celestial visitors.

The prophet Daniel, while in vision, saw the throne of God where "thousands ministered unto him, and ten thousand times ten thousand stood before him" (Daniel 7:10). David, the sweet singer of Israel, declares that when Jehovah proclaimed His law at Mt. Sinai, there were present "thousands of angels" (Psalm 68:17).

Literally countless millions of angels are ever ready and eager to obey the commands of their divine Leader. And every true child of God has the promise: "He shall give his angels charge over thee, to keep thee in all thy ways" (Psalm 91:11).

* * *

Think of it, fathers and mothers, your children, your sons and your daughters, can and will enjoy the constant and ever watchful vigilance of these heavenly beings in answer to your earnest prayers in their behalf. Whether your loved ones are at work, or traveling over land or sea, whether peacefully pursuing their daily task, or on the field of battle, night and day, in every place and clime, angels, who neither slumber nor sleep, attend their steps, never slackening their tireless vigil, nor growing weary of their tender solicitude.

These heavenly angels are designated in the Bible as "ministering spirits," because they are commissioned of God to minister to His children. They comfort, guide, and protect those who serve Him.

Angels are constantly bearing the prayers of the needy and distressed to the Father above, and bring blessing and hope, courage and help, to the children of men.

We have a vivid illustration of this in the experience of the patriarch Jacob. He had taken unfair advantage of his brother Esau in order to obtain the birthright, and he had deceived his father in order to obtain his blessing. Threatened with death by the wrath of Esau, Jacob left his father's home as a fugitive. The darkness of despair pressed upon his soul, and he hardly dared to pray. Yet in his utter loneliness he felt the need of divine protection as he had never felt it before. With bitter weeping and deep humiliation he confessed his sin, and pleaded for some evidence that God had not utterly forsaken him. As he slept, he dreamed: "And behold a ladder set up on the earth, and the top of it reached to heaven: and behold the angels of God ascending and descending on it. And behold, the Lord stood above it" (Genesis 28:12, 13).

Jacob awakened with a sense of the abiding presence of God. Strengthened in faith, and with the full assurance of the guardianship of heavenly angels, he pursued his journey.

Angels from the courts above will just as surely attend the steps of the humble, repentant child of God today, as they did in ancient times.

What about Elijah's experience? Probably none of us ever had a more disheartening and discouraging experience than Elijah the prophet, who fled for his life before the threatened vengeance of the wicked and infuriated queen Jezebel. Forgetting God, he fled on and on, until he found himself all alone in a desolate, dreary wilderness, far from the dwelling places of men. His spirit crushed by bitter disappointment, he requested that he might die. "It is enough, now O Lord," he pleaded, "Take away my life; for I am not better than my fathers" (I Kings 19:4).

Did Jehovah forget his tried and tested servant? Did He take him at his word and permit him to die in the wilderness? Indeed not! Angels were commissioned to encourage, comfort, and sustain him.

Into the experience of all there come times of deep disappointment and utter discouragement—days when sorrow is the portion, and it is hard to believe that the Lord God is still the kind benefactor of His earthborn children; days when troubles harass the soul, till death seems preferable to life. It is then that men lose their hold on God, and are brought into the slavery of doubt, the bondage of unbelief with its terrible consequences. Could we at such times discern with spiritual insight the meaning of God's providences, we should see angels seeking to save us from ourselves, striving to plant our feet upon a foundation more firm than the everlasting hills, and new faith, new life, would spring into being. I know we all feel lonely, inadequate and forsaken at times. Many times we are a victim of adverse circumstances! But, we need not despair. As we turn to the Lord Jesus and by faith and prayer take hold of the precious promises found in His word, God will change, wonderfully change the most hopeless, discouraging outlook. And our guardian angels, though unseen by us, will whisper hope, and cheer, encouraging us to walk in the straight and narrow way, the way of righteousness, the way to God's heart!

And as we order our lives in harmony with God's unerring guide, the Bible, we will some day, in a better world, namely, in God's eternal kingdom, be privileged to meet the angels who guided us through life's thorny way; who were with us in the valley of the shadow of death; who marked our resting place, and who were the first to greet us in the resurrection morning. O, what joy will it be to hold converse with those celestial beings, and to learn from them the full and complete story of divine guidance in our individual lives!

From what dangers, visible and invisible, we have been preserved through the interposition of the angels, we shall never know, until in the light of eternity we see the providences of God. Then we shall know that the whole heavenly family of God was interested in the family here below, and that messengers from the throne of God attended our steps from day to day.

As we review our past, and discern the precious evidences of God's protecting care and of the work of His angels in our behalf, let us thank and praise God for His loving-kindness and tender mercy. Let us resolve to study His word, the Bible, thoughtfully and prayerfully, that we may carry out its beneficent principles and precepts in our daily life. In so doing we shall have the constant companionship of these celestial visitants—the holy angels—who delight to do God's will and who linger and abide where His Word is studied, cherished, and obeyed in the hearts of we children of men!

8

The Character of Satan

THE CHARACTER OF SATAN

The Bible tells us that there is a real devil and that he, Satan, was once a commanding angel in heaven. Notice the words we read in the Bible recorded in Isaiah 14:12-14: "How art thou fallen from heaven, O Lucifer, son of the morning! how art thou cut down to the ground, which didst weaken the nations! For thou hast said in thine heart, I will ascend into heaven, I will exalt my throne above the stars of God: I will sit also upon the mount of the congregation, in the sides of the north: I will ascend above the heights of the clouds; I will be like the Most High."

Here the fact is disclosed that Lucifer was once a leader in heaven, and was cast out of heaven because he rebelled against God. Five times he used the word "I" in exalting himself before the other angels. Notice his words:

"I will ascend into heaven,

"I will exalt my throne above the stars of God:

"I will sit also upon the mount of the congregation, in the sides of the north:

"I will ascend above the heights of the clouds;

"I will be like the Most High."

Imagine, if you will, the audacity of this angel trying to make himself like God and going so far as to say, "I shall be like the Most High." Then God goes on to explain that all of our sorrows and troubles in this world are due to this wicked angel who made of himself a devil. The Lord says: "Yet thou shalt be brought down to hell, to the sides of the pit. They that see thee shall narrowly look upon thee and consider thee, saying, Is this man that made the earth to tremble, that did shake kingdoms: that made the world as a wilderness, and destroyed the cities thereof; that opened not the house of his prisoners?" (Isaiah 14:15-17).

Here we are told that Satan has caused the earth to tremble. Who will deny that Satan has caused great agitation among the nations of the earth? He did "shake the kingdoms." It is he that causes war and that destroys cities and nations. It is he that causes death, and the Bible says, "Opened not the house of his prisoners."

Inasmuch as Satan was once a commanding angel in heaven, he would of course have been created the same as all the other angels. The messages of Ezekiel 28:12-19 are generally regarded as referring to the king of Tyre, first as a historical personage, and second, as a type of the devil prior to his expulsion from the presence of God. In Ezekiel 28:15 God says: "Thou wast perfect in thy ways from the day thou wast created, till iniquity was found in thee." So here we have the record that Satan was perfect in his ways from the day that he was created until iniquity, or sin, entered into his life.

To show how he once was in the presence of God in heaven, we read Ezekiel 28:13: "Thou hast been in Eden the garden of God; every precious stone was thy covering, the sardius, topaz, and the diamond, the beryl, the onyx, and the jasper, the sapphire, the emerald, and the carbuncle, and gold: the workmanship of thy tabrets and of thy pipes was in thee; in the day that thou was created they were prepared."

One of the highest order of angels in heaven are the cherubim, and Lucifer was the leader, because the Bible points out that he was one of the cherubim that covered the mercy seat of God. Notice in Ezekiel 28:14: "Thou art the anointed cherub that covereth; and I have set thee so: thou wast upon the holy mountain of God; thou hast walked up and down in the midst of the stones of fire."

Referring again as to why Lucifer was evicted from heaven, we read in Ezekiel 28:16: "By the multitude of thy merchandise they have filled the midst of thee with violence, and *thou hast sinned: therefore I will cast thee as profane out of the mountain of God:* and I will destroy thee, O covering cherub, from the midst of the stones of fire."

Because sin had entered into this angel's life, God could no longer tolerate him in heaven, and he was cast out into the earth where he causes man to sin. Thus a great struggle confronts every person as to whom he shall choose to serve. Those following the teachings of the New Birth shall be found among the justified. Those who disregard the teachings of Jesus and continue in unregenerate sins, automatically become servants of Satan and will not share in the eternal life offered to all ages in Christ Jesus.

*   *   *

Once more turning to the book of Ezekiel we read that the Lord says: "Thou art the seal of perfection full of wisdom, and perfect in beauty.... Thine heart was lifted up because of thy beauty, thou hast corrupted thy wisdom by reason of thy brightness: I will cast thee to the ground, and I will lay thee before kings, that they may behold thee" (Ezekiel 28:12, 17).

Here we learn that Lucifer was perfect in beauty. Some people picture the devil as being red, having horns, split hoofs, spiked tail, with fire coming out of his nostrils, and a pitchfork in his hands. Satan would like us to believe that he looked like this; but rather, as we have just noticed from the Bible, he was *perfect in beauty* and the first thing that he did when he came to this world was to cause man to sin.

After Satan was cast out of heaven, we find him in the garden of Eden, where Adam and Eve were dwelling. Instead of coming as a wicked angel, he used a serpent as his medium of communication. Some Jewish theologians believe that the serpent originally was a beautiful creature, and inasmuch as we find the serpent in the tree, presume that it was once a beautiful bird; however, this is a conjecture. We know that Satan had used the serpent for his subtle deception, God cursed the serpent and said: "Because thou hast done this, thou art cursed above all cattle, and above every beast of the field; upon thy belly shalt thou go, and dust shalt thou eat all the days of thy life" (Genesis 3:14).

Appearing in the form of a serpent Satan awaited the right opportunity, perhaps when Eve would stray by alone. We find recorded in Genesis 3:1-6 the conversation that ensued between Satan and the woman Eve: "Now the serpent was more subtle than any beast of the field which the Lord God had made. And he said unto the woman, Yea, hath God said, Ye shall not eat of every tree of the garden? And the woman said unto the serpent, We may eat of the fruit of trees of the garden: But of the fruit of the tree which is in the midst of the garden, God hath said, Ye shall not eat of it, neither shall ye touch it, lest ye die. And the serpent said unto the woman, Ye shall not surely die: For God doth know that in the day ye eat thereof, then your eyes shall be opened, and ye shall be as gods, knowing good and evil. And when the woman saw that the tree was good for food, and that it was pleasant to the eyes, and a tree to be desired to make one wise, she took of the fruit thereof, and did eat, and gave also unto her husband with her; and he did eat."

Even though Adam and Eve had been warned that if they ate thereof they would surely die, yet they disobeyed God, through temptation of the devil, and thus sin entered the world. But Satan has not stopped his temptations, for he and the wicked angels, his followers that were cast out of heaven with him, are constantly tempting man to sin.

*   *   *

To show further how this is done, let us refer you to the Scripture as recorded in Job 1:1—2:10. We suggest you read the entire passage of which we quote only a few verses: "There was a man in the land of Uz, whose name was Job and that man was perfect and upright, and one that feared God, and eschewed evil. Now there was a day when the sons of God came to present themselves before the Lord, and Satan came along also among them. And the Lord said unto Satan, Whence comest thou? Then Satan answered the Lord, and said, From going to and fro in the earth, and from walking up and down in it. And the Lord said unto Satan, Hast thou considered my servant Job, that there is none like him in the earth, a perfect and an upright man, one that feareth God, and escheweth evil? Then Satan answered the Lord and said, Doth Job fear God for nought? Hast not thou made an hedge about him, and about his house, and about all that he hath on every side? thou hast blessed the work of his hands, and his substance is increased in the land. But put forth thine hand now, and touch all that he hath, and he will curse thee to thy face. And the Lord said unto Satan, Behold, all that he hath is in thy power, only upon himself put not forth thine hand. So Satan went forth from the presence of the Lord.

"Again there was a day when the sons of God came to present themselves before the Lord, and Satan came also among them to present himself before the Lord. And the Lord said unto Satan, From whence comest thou? And Satan answered the Lord and said, From going to and fro in the earth, walking up and down in it. And the Lord said unto Satan, Hast thou considered my servant Job, that there is none like him in the earth, a perfect and upright man, one that feareth God, and escheweth evil? and still he holdeth fast his integrity, although thou movedst me against him, to destroy him without cause. And Satan answered the Lord, and said, Skin for skin, all that a man hath will he give for his life. But put forth thine hand now, and touch his bone and his flesh, and he will curse thee to thy face. And the Lord said unto Satan, Behold, he is in thine hand; but save his life. So went Satan forth from the presence of the Lord, and smote Job with sore boils from the sole of his foot unto his crown."

* * *

To learn how Satan tempts man to sin, we have only to read the account of how King David was tempted of the devil to number Israel, something which God had forbidden. We read of this in I Chronicles:

"And Satan stood against Israel, and provoked David to number Israel. And David said to Joab and the princes of the people: Go, number Israel from Beersheba even to Dan....And Joab said: ...Why will he be a cause of guilt unto Israel? Nevertheless the king's word prevailed against Joab. Wherefore Joab departed, and went throughout all Israel and came to Jerusalem....And God sent an angel unto Jerusalem to destroy it; and as he was about to destroy, the Lord beheld, and he repented him of the evil, and said to the destroying angel: It is enough; now stay thy hand. And the angel of the Lord was standing by the threshing floor of Ornan the Jebusite....And David said unto God: Is it not I that commanded the people to be numbered? even I it is that have sinned and done very wickedly...let thy hand, I pray thee, O Lord my God, be against me, and against my father's house; but not against thy people, that they should be plagued....And David built there an altar unto the Lord, and offered burnt offerings and called upon the Lord; and he answered him from heaven by fire upon the altar of burnt-offering. And the Lord commanded the angel; and he put up his sword back into the sheath thereof."

* * *

Some may wonder why God did not kill Lucifer as soon as he sinned against God. The question arises, Why does God permit the devil to live and cause so much sorrow and suffering? But this is very easily answered when we stop to realize that Satan made an accusation against God, and had God killed him immediately, all the universe would have worshipped God in fear. To illustrate this, let us think about Satan accusing God before all the angels. Telling them that God was unjust, that God was a tyrant, and trying to inspire the unfallen angels to come over on his side, he made many accusations which were untrue. So when the day arrived that God could no longer tolerate him and those who sided with him in heaven, He cast them out of heaven and into the earth. But, had God killed the devil and the wicked angels that followed him, all of the good angels, and all the inhabitants of the unfallen worlds that know no sin would have worshipped God in fear, instead of love. They would have said, "Satan is right, God is unjust." Hence God has permitted Satan to carry on his devilish work for thousands of years as an object lesson to the entire creation, thus demonstrating that disobedience to God's plan of salvation results in misery, suffering, sorrow, and finally death. However, Satan's reign of sin, according to theological interpretation, is to be terminated. God has given him ample opportunity to show himself in his true colors before all the universe. He has about completed his cup of iniquity to the full. God's justice has been completely vindicated. The accusations Satan made against God have turned upon his own head. Therefore with the eradication of Satan from men's lives God will cleanse the heart from its defilement, degradation and satanic corruption.

*   *   *

To show how God is to eradicate Satan, sin and eventually the unrepentant sinner, let us read Zephaniah 3:14-17: "Sing, O daughter of Zion; shout, O Israel; be glad and rejoice with all the heart, O daughter of Jerusalem. The Lord hath taken away thy judgments, he hath cast out thine enemy [Satan]: the King of Israel, even the Lord, is in the midst of thee: thou shalt not see evil any more. In that day it shall be said to Jerusalem, Fear thou not: and to Zion, Let not thine hands be slack. The Lord thy God in the midst of thee is mighty; he will save, he will rejoice over thee with joy; he will rest in his love, he will joy over thee with singing."

Read for yourself the beautiful words found in Isaiah 65:17-19, 24 and Isaiah 66:22, 23. Even though Satan is the enemy of man and the enemy of Jehovah, and His word, the Bible, yet God is long suffering, and in due time He is going to destroy the devil, his wicked angels, and all wicked people who insist in worshiping after him. And then He will create a new heaven, a new earth, wherein dwelleth righteousness, with no sin and no devil to tempt us.

To show how Jehovah is going to destroy the devil, let us read Ezekiel 28:18, 19: "Thou hast defiled thy sanctuaries by the multitude of thine iniquities, by the iniquity of thy traffic; therefore will I bring forth a fire from the midst of thee, it shall devour thee, and I will bring thee to ashes upon the earth in the sight of all them that behold thee. All they that know thee among the people shall be astonished at thee; thou shalt be a terror, and never shalt thou be any more."

These are striking and hopeful words Jehovah has spoken concerning the devil when he predicted: *"I will bring thee to ashes... and never shalt thou be any more."*

In Malachi 4:1, 3 we read how the Lord God is going to deal with Satan, sin, and sinners: "For behold, the day cometh, that shall burn as an oven; and all the proud, yea, and all that do wickedly, shall be stubble; and the day that cometh shall burn them up, saith the Lord of Hosts, that it shall leave them neither root nor branch. And ye shall tread down the wicked; for they shall be ashes under the soles of your feet in the day that I shall prepare, saith the Lord of hosts."

*   *   *

However, let us remember that God has no pleasure in the death of the wicked. He tells us so in Ezekiel 33:11: "For behold, I create new heavens and a new earth: and the former shall not be remembered, nor come into mind. But be ye glad and rejoice for ever in that which I create: for, behold, I create Jerusalem a rejoicing, and her people a joy. And I will rejoice in Jerusalem, and joy in my people: and the voice of weeping shall be no more heard in her, nor the voice of crying....And it shall come to pass, that before they call, I will answer, and while they are yet speaking, I will hear....For as the new heavens and the new earth, which I will make, shall remain before me, saith the Lord so shall your seed and your name remain. And it shall come to pass, that from one new moon to another, and from one Sabbath to another, shall all flesh come to worship me, saith the Lord."

Each morning when we awake from our sleep, we should pray to the God of heaven to keep us that day free from temptation of the devil, and ask Him to lead us by His grace. David the psalmist, illustrates a beautiful prayer when he prayed in Psalm 23:

"The Lord is my shepherd; I shall not want. He maketh me to lie down in green pastures: he leadeth me beside the still waters. He restoreth my soul: he leadeth me in the paths of righteousness for his name's sake. Yea, though I walk through the valley of the shadow of death, I will fear no evil: for thou art with me; thy rod and thy staff they comfort me. Thou preparest a table before me in the presence of mine enemies: thou anointest my head with oil; my cup runneth over. Surely goodness and mercy shall follow me all the days of my life: and I will dwell in the house of the Lord for ever."

9

Ancient History

ANCIENT HISTORY

The Bible is unique in its excellence. Among the countless literary productions it stands alone. No other book compares with the Bible in the universality and timelessness of its appeal and persuasiveness. Although its several books were transcribed mostly by writers of but one nationality, the Hebrews, yet the influence of the Bible extends to every nation on the face of the earth. Despite the fact that it was completed many centuries ago, it is never out of date, and is still the "best seller" by a wide margin. It is as fresh as today's headlines. To this day its vitality and its power to transform and regenerate men's hearts are undiminished.

While the Bible excels all other books in many ways, it is in the field of prophecy that it shines with a far-reaching luster. It is the only book which forecasts future events, speaking of them with even greater definiteness than does many a historian when referring to ancient and immediately past history. Its prophetic pronouncements constitute incontrovertible evidence of its divine origin. The man who reads a Bible prophecy and sees its fulfillment in a corresponding event, is himself the witness of the miracle. It is on this point the theology challenges infidels and agnostics to demonstrate their superior wisdom. Says the prophet Isaiah: "Declare us things ...to come. Show [or tell] the things that are to come hereafter, that we may know that ye are gods" (Isaiah 41:22, 23).

The following Old Testament texts emphasize this outstanding feature of the Bible—that of accurately foretelling the future:

"Remember the former things of old: for I am God, and there is none else; I am God, and there is none like me, Declaring the end from the beginning, and from ancient times the things that are not yet done" (Isaiah 46:9, 10).

"Surely the Lord God will do nothing, but he revealeth his secret unto his servants the prophets" (Amos 3:7).

Scores and hundreds of prophecies affecting countries, governments, cities, and individuals are found in the Scriptures. Oh, that men might learn the inestimable value of prophecy, for it is like a beacon light which points the way to security and peace amid the darkness and uncertainty of this atomic age.

It is said that an infidel French ruler on a certain occasion challenged a believer to produce one outstanding evidence that the Scriptures were inspired. The pious man replied: "The Jew." And indeed, the Hebrew people are a perpetual and a living testimony to the truthfulness and accuracy of Bible prophecy.

The origin and development of the Hebrew race were revealed to Abraham, their progenitor, when the divine command came to this man of faith to leave his father's house, and go to a strange land. In bidding Abraham to sever his family ties, the Lord made this prophetic promise: "And I will make of thee a great nation, and I will bless thee, and make thy name great; and thou shalt be a blessing" (Genesis 12:2).

When this promise was made, Abraham was at an advanced age, and childless, with no reasonable prospect that children would be born to him. Nevertheless, the promise was fulfilled, for not only does the literal seed of Abraham number millions, but we find the name of Abraham so renowned, that hundreds of millions of Christains and Mohammedans speak of him with the utmost reverence.

An outstanding prophecy concerning the condition of the Hebrew people for the past two millenniums, is recorded in the writings of Moses. As the Holy Spirit gave Moses a look into the distant future, he saw, and then described, what would be the history of the Hebrew nation: "And the Lord shall scatter thee among all people, from the one end of the earth even unto the other" (Deuteronomy 28:64).

The past twenty centuries have been the accurate fulfillment of this prediction. The scattered fragments of the Hebrew people among the nations of the world today, are an ever-present testimony to the truthfulness of prophetic Bible utterance. Great and powerful empires of antiquity have disappeared, but the children of Abraham still maintain their existence, even though they have endured merciless persecution, and have been circumscribed, ostracized, and exiled from country to country. Their racial longevity and marvelous endurance are a source of wonder and astonishment among the nations. There is scarcely a country or a city anywhere on earth, but that among its citizens may be found one or more representatives of this peculiar and vigorous race.

Many a less virile race has amalgamated with other nations, and in time entirely lost its identity. It is not so with the Hebrew people. To this day most Jews retain the racial and traditional characteristics which distinguish them from all other people. Thus every son or daughter of Abraham we meet is a living witness to the truthfulness and accuracy of this Bible prophecy.

* * *

Also, there is the prophecy concerning Babylon. Every high school student is familiar with the history of the once great empire of Babylon. Her capital city, one of the wonders of the world, with its luxuriant pleasure-grounds and gardens, and its two royal palaces, was rightly called "the golden city of a golden age." In it was the imposing temple of Belus and the beautiful hanging gardens piled high in successive terraces. Its great walls towered upwards of two hundred feet, and were so wide on the top as to enable several chariots to race side by side. It contained enough provisions to enable it to resist a besieging army, if necessary, for twenty years. Proud, luxurious, boastful, and sinful Babylon was the mistress of the world.

But while Babylon was in the heyday of its glory and pomp, the Hebrew prophet Isaiah, was commanded of the Lord to make the following bold prediction concerning that world metropolis:

"Babylon, the glory of kingdoms, the beauty of the Chaldees' excellency, shall be as when God overthrew Sodom and Gomorrah. It shall *never be inhabited,* neither shall it be dwelt in from generation to generation: neither shall the Abrabian pitch tent there; neither shall the shepherds make their fold there.

"And the wild beasts of the islands shall cry in their desolate houses, and dragons in their pleasant palaces: and her time is near to come, and her days shall not be prolonged" (Isaiah 13:19-22).

Where is Babylon today? Belshazzar, her last reigning monarch, was conquered and slain by the Medo-Persian soldiers in the year 538 B.C., one hundred and fifty years after the fatal prediction was made by the prophet. For centuries the city of Babylon has been a vast heap of ruins—a desolation; it has not been inhabited. In its present desolate condition, Babylon is a standing challenge to all skeptics and infidels.

The prophet Jeremiah made the following additional prediction concerning Babylon: "Chaldea [Babylon] shall be a spoil: all that spoil her shall be satisfied, saith the Lord. . . . Come against her from the utmost border, open her storehouses. . . and destroy her utterly" (Jeremiah 50:10, 26).

History verifies the fulfillment of this marvelous prophecy. No other city was so frequently looted, and robbed of its apparently inexhaustible riches as was Babylon. Cyrus, Xerxes, Alexander of Macedon, the Parthians, and the Romans successively despoiled that wondrous city. It became the prey of every conqueror.

*   *   *

The prophecy concerning Egypt is in contrast to all the afore-mentioned prophecy, and it is interesting and illuminating to note what the divine Forecaster said concerning the land of the Pharaohs: "And I will bring again the captivity of Egypt, and will cause them to return into the land of Pathros, into the land of their habitation; and they shall be there a base kingdom. It shall be the basest of the kingdoms; neither shall it exalt itself any more above the nations; for I will diminish them, that they shall no more rule over the nations" (Ezekiel 29:14, 15).

This singular prediction was made about the year 600 B.C., when Egypt was a dominating empire, the granary of the world, the mother of sciences, literature, and art, a land justly famed for her pyramids. From all human appearances, her power and magnificence could have been maintained forever, but the prophet, foreseeing the diminishing of her excellence, declares that she would become the "basest," or most insignificant of kingdoms. Mark the prophet's words; she was not to be utterly destroyed as was Babylon, but was to continue to exist, although shorn of her former power. How seemingly daring was the prophecy, and how striking the fulfillment!

The infidel Volney in his *"Travels,"* Vol. 1, pp. 74, 103, 110, 193, says in part: "Such is the state of Egypt, Deprived two thousand three hundred years ago of her natural proprietors, she   has seen her fertile fields successively a prey to the Persians, the Macedon-ians, the Romans, the Greeks, the Arabs. . .and at length the race of Tartars, distinguished by the name of Ottoman Turks. The Mamelukes, purchased as slaves, and introduced as soldiers, soon usurped the power, and elected a leader. . . .Everything the traveler sees or hears reminds him he is in the country of slavery and tyranny."

No human sagacity could possibly have foreseen these events as recorded in the Bible. Let us suppose that the prophet, Ezekiel, had said that Egypt was to be utterly destroyed like Babylon, or vice versa? How jubilant the enemies of the Bible would be, now triumphant in their boasting to disprove Bible prophecy! While the Scriptures contain hundreds of predictions, not one of them failed, nor can it ever fail. (See Kings 8:56.)

*   *   *

Now let us examine the prophecy concerning Tyre. The city of Tyre on the Mediterranean coast was the New York of ancient Asia. Ships from all nations anchored in her harbor, and their passengers bartered in her streets. But at the height of her power and glory, the prophet Ezekiel stated in 590 B.C., that the proud, godless city would be overthrown, and utterly destroyed, and that the very dust of her streets would be scraped, and that she would become like the top of a rock: "It shall be a place for the spreading of nets in the midst of the sea: for I have spoken it, saith the Lord God:...and they shall lay thy stones and thy timber and thy dust in the midst of the water....I will make thee like the top of a rock: thou shalt be a place to spread nets upon; thou shalt be built no more; for I the Lord have spoken it, saith the Lord God" (Ezekiel 26:5, 12-14).

The very name of the man (Nebuchadnezzar) and the name of the power (Babylon) which should overthrow the city were foretold. (See Ezekiel 26:7-9.)

Shortly after this prophecy was uttered, Nebuchadnezzar, the king of Babylon, laid siege to Tyre. After thirteen years of effort, he captured the city, and utterly destroyed it. The city was left in ruins. But the prophet had said that the very dust of the city would be scraped, and that it would become like the top of a rock. Two centuries and a half passed and the ruins still remained untouched, a challenge to the accuracy of God's word. A new city of Tyre had been built on an island half a mile away from the former site, and the inhabitants had hoped that the surging waters of the Mediterranean would shield them from the attacks of any future invader. But in the year 332 B.C., Alexander the Great swept down the shores of the Mediterranean, and in order to reach the new city of Tyre, tore down the walls, towers, and timbers of the ruined houses and palaces of ancient Tyre, and with them built a solid causeway in the midst of the old ruins in order to supply the demand for the necessary material. To this day the ancient city has not been rebuilt; and local fishermen spread their nets on the rocks of the seashore, exactly as was foretold by the prophet many centuries ago. What a truly, marvelous fulfillment! Only divine foreknowledge and wisdom could make such a series of accurate predictions.

*   *   *

Of course there are a number of other prophecies in the Old and New Testaments. Space does not permit the quoting of a large number of other prophecies just as specific as the ones we have considered, and just as convincing. The pages of the Bible abound in forecasts concerning Jerusalem, Judea, the twelve tribes of Israel, Samaria, Philistia, Moab, Gaza, Chaldea, Syria, Nineveh, Medo-Persia, Greece, etc. Many of these prophecies have already been fulfilled, while others are in the process of being fulfilled.

For decades higher critics and infidel authors endeavored to discredit the Bible, claiming that some of its historical references to peoples and nations were mere legends, inasmuch as no ancient documents could be found to verify their historicity.

These Bible detractors grew bolder with the years, until in the eyes of professor and students, and even of some theologians, the Bible was nothing more or less than a collection of mythological tales. However, a change came in 1799 when the famous Rosetta stone was discovered not far from the mouth of the Nile, and its Egyptian inscriptions were deciphered by the French scholar Champollion in 1822. Thus he provided a key which unlocked the secrets of the treasures of ancient Egypt and other oriental nations.

Archaeology was given a tremendous impetus. The stones began to cry out and their testimony was illuminating. Every document unearthed served but to vindicate the truths of the Bible, and, incidentally, to put its critics to shame. Many honest doubters cast their quibbles aside, and instead became enthusiastic defenders of the infallibility of the Scriptures. We quote from a well-known scientist and archeologist, Professor A. H. Sayce: "Recent discoveries have retorted the critic's objections upon himself. It is not the Bible writer, but the modern author who is proved to have been unacquainted with the contemporaneous history of the time" (Quoted from *The Hittites, The Story of a Forgotten People,* page 12).

It has been truthfully said that the Scriptures are as an anvil which has worn out many a hammer. The Bible has been refuted, demolished, overthrown, and exploded more times than any other book you ever heard of....Every now and then somebody starts up and upsets this book; but it is like upsetting a solid cube of granite. It is just as big one way as the other; and when it is upset, it is right side up, and when it is overturned again, it is right side up still....For a book that has been exploded so many times, this book is still very much alive.

The Bible tells us where we are today in the procession of the ages, and what may be expected in time to come. Much of what prophecy has foretold we can trace on the pages of history; and we may be assured the rest will be fulfilled in its order.

Amid all the constantly changing theories, speculations, and human opinions, the Bible alone knows no change. Like its divine Author, it is the same yesterday, today, and forever.

"All flesh is grass, and all the goodliness thereof, is as the flower of the field:...The grass withereth, the flower fadeth:...but the word of our God shall stand forever" (Isaiah 40:6, 8).

As a Christian you should never cease to make the Bible your counselor, the rule of your daily life. It not only presents a perfect standard of character, but it is also an infallible guide under all circumstances and conditions, leading in paths of truth and righteousness to the very end of life's journey.

* * *

For many centuries the printing of books was a slow, costly, and laborious process. Only the rich could afford to have them. Newspapers were small in size, and many hours were required in the printing of a small edition. In our day, an entire Sunday edition of two million copies of a cosmopolitan daily is printed, folded, and counted in about five hours. It would have taken Benjamin Franklin, the founder of the *Saturday Evening Post*, two thousand years to turn out such a Sunday edition with his old hand press. Recently a tree was cut down in the suburbs of a large city at 7:35 a.m. It was converted into woodpulp, out of which a roll of paper was made ready for the printing press by 9:35 a.m. At 10 o'clock the same forenoon, the newsboys were selling the finished product of the tree which had blossomed in the suburb of that city only two hours and twenty-five minutes earlier!

Have you ever thought about the reason for these wonders of wonders? Some thoughtful, inquiring person might raise the question as to the significance of these wonders, and why these amazing discoveries and time and laborsaving devices have all been crowded into this present century? The answer is: first, that our faith might be established in regard to the prophetic portions of God's word; and second, that God might all the more quickly accomplish His beneficient designs in behalf of the human race.

We are living in "the time of the end." The Lord's coming is at hand! This is the only panacea for the world's ills. In order that all the inhabitants of the earth might have an opportunity to prepare for this climactic event, the good news of His coming must be proclaimed in all the world. This takes consecrated preachers, teachers, evangelists and missionaries.

One hundred years ago there were no facilities for the giving of God's message to all the world in a single generation. The Bible was scarce and expensive. Very few had access to it. It was printed in but few languages, and there were few agencies to promote its circulation. Its wide dissemination was impossible one hundred years ago, inasmuch as there were no means of easy and rapid communication or transportation between people and the governments.

Today, Bible and Tract societies are printing the Scriptures in more than a thousand languages and dialects, and the Word of God is speedily being carried to earth's remotest bounds by steamship, by train, and by airplane. Even the natives of the African jungles and those of the islands of the Pacific can now read the Bible in their own tongues. Since we are living in uncertain and troublous times, God has so ordered events as to bring the Bible within easy reach of all classes of people in every land and climate, that all may have the opportunity to prepare for the most momentous event of history, namely, the imminent coming of the Lord Jesus. Soon every one will have heard God's last warning message, and when it has done its appointed work, "then shall the end come." Of course nobody knows the actual date of this event. We should not frustrate ourselves as to time, etc.

*   *   *

What about the moral condition of this age? The question might well be asked: Has this generation advanced morally in proportion to the intellectual progress it has made? Is the average man and woman of today of stronger moral fiber than were our forefathers of a century ago? At one time our educators informed us that all that this world needed in order to make it a veritable Utopia, was education, and more education, knowledge, and more knowledge. God, however, foresaw the moral degeneracy of the human race and the destructive uses to which it would put its scientific discoveries, and He, therefore, mercifully withheld from man a knowledge of the hidden powers and forces of nature until this last generation.

Chancellor Arthur H. Compton, of Washington University, St. Louis, Mo., who directed research at the University of Chicago as dean of the Physical Sciences division, quoted Winston Churchill as saying: "This revelation of the facts of nature long mercifully withheld from man should arouse the most solemn reflections in the minds and conscience of every human being. We must pray that these awful agencies [hydrogen bombs, etc.] will be made to conduce peace among nations, and instead of wreaking measureless havoc upon the entire globe, that they may become a perennial foundation of world prosperity" (Quoted from *The Chicago Sun* August 9, 1945).

In a recent reprint of *This Week,* newspaper supplement of May 7, 1944, famed Russian-born Major Alexander P. deSeversky, who had much to do with building lethal weapons of the air in World War II, warned us as to what we may expect in the very near future. We quote: "The nations of the world hold in their hands scientific force capable of blowing all civilization to bits....In the wars of the immediate future entire populations will be directly menaced by the instruments of demolition more effective than any now in existence....The destructive power of electronics, the lethal resources of modern chemistry, have scarcely been tapped. Within a decade or less, they will be ready to visit horror on man in new and almost unimagined forms....No ocean barriers, no defensive weapons are effective safeguards against the destructive forces being used at this very minute. They will be utterly worthless against the annihilation that will be loosed tomorrow."

These facts make it evident that unless the Saviour hastens His coming, the destructive forces which modern science is even now perfecting in the laboratories of the world, soon may wipe us all off the earth. At least we are told and believe the possibility of such a predicament. Man has the physical potential to destroy civilization as we know it today.

That the Saviour's coming and the end of the present evil world may be sooner than anticipated is indicated by prevailing conditions. This generation has well-nigh filled up its cup of iniquity.

Uprightness, goodness and justice are rapidly disappearing, while hatred, greed, and lust are supplanting every moral virtue. One great Apostle gives us a most startling and yet realistic portrayal of this generation. We quote: "This know also that in the last days perilous times shall come. For men shall be lovers of their own selves, covetous, boasters, proud, blasphemers, disobedient to parents, unthankful, unholy, without natural affection, truce-breakers, false accusers, incontinent, fierce, despisers of those that are good, traitors, heady, high-minded, lovers of pleasures more than lovers of God" (II Timothy 3:1-4).

The wickedness prevailing in our day, according to revealed theology, is similar to that which existed before the flood in Noah's day. The antediluvians lost their fear of God, and cast off all restraint. They ridiculed the idea of personal accountability, or of a judgment day. They ignored and wilfully broke the love of God, and defied their Creator. God repeatedly warned them of the impending judgment, and gave them ample time in which to repent and to mend their wicked ways. But they mocked Noah, and despised the heaven-sent messages of warning, until the flood finally came and took them all away. We are told that so shall it also be in the last generation.

Are we ready for the Saviour's second coming? Every invention of this age, every speeding automobile, every roar of the jet planes, and the innumerable contrivances, the thousand and one push-button conveniences, and devices which are so rapidly multiplying on every hand, all speak to us in thunder tones that, "the end of all things is at hand." History is rapidly being fulfilled before our very eyes.

"Time is short!" "The great day of the Lord is near, it is near, and hasteth greatly" (Zephaniah 1:14). Therefore—"prepare to meet thy God" (Amos 4:12). Trust in Jesus—trust Him NOW!

10

The Holy Scriptures

THE HOLY SCRIPTURES

A large part of the earth's children study, revere, live and worship by a book that is essentially God's book, namely, the Bible. Its vast contribution to the physical, moral, and spiritual well-being of mankind, and its influence and impact upon the course of human history, can never be fully computed. This "Book of books" is interwoven into the very fabric of our modern civilization. All that is humane, majestic, illustrious in modern government, education, and jurisprudence, is due either directly or indirectly to the teachings of the Holy Scriptures. It is this infiltration of the Bible into modern society that distinguishes our day from the Dark Ages when the Bible was suppressed and its circulation and reading were forbidden under pain of incarceration, torture, and death. The concepts of liberty, equality, and fraternity, now well nigh universally accepted, were practiced by the children of Israel thousands of years ago, when Moses was bidden by the God of heaven to "proclaim liberty throughout all the land unto all the inhabitants thereof" (Leviticus 25:10).

Translated into hundreds of languages, printed in thousands of editions, and circulated by the hundreds of millions of copies, the Bible has gone to every nation on earth, and its words unto the end of the world. Wherever the Scriptures are most widespread and held in the highest esteem, there, democratic principles, true culture and enlightenment are most firmly entrenched.

The term "Bible" comes from the Greek word *biblos,* meaning a book. The Bible, however, is more than just a book; it is composed of many books, integrated and permeated by one grand and absorbing theme — God's boundless love for mankind.

Among its divinely inspired writers are Moses, a legislator and leader; David and Solomon, kings of Israel; Nehemiah, a cup bearer to the Persian king; Ezra, the scribe; Daniel, the Prime Minister of Babylon; Amos, a herdsman; Ezekiel, a priest, etc. Men of varied social levels, occupations, capabilities and talents are among the authors of this amazing book that speaks with authority and unimpeachable accuracy on such subjects as history, genealogy, ethnology, law, ethics, prophecy, medicine, sanitary science, and political economy. It contains perfect rules of conduct for the guidance of the individual as well as of society, and fairly bristles with gems of poetry and eloquence unsurpassed in all literature in all civilizations.

The first five books of the Bible, known as the Pentateuch, were written by Moses some thirty-five centuries ago. Over eighteen centuries have elapsed since the Bible was completed, and yet it is read, studied, obeyed, and loved by more people in this reputedly sophisticated age, than in any other period of this world's history. Other books, written by uninspired men, are soon out of date and in time become obsolete. For instance, Plato's or Aristotle's dissertations on medicine now only provoke a smile. Even many of our modern textbooks need constant changing and revising in order to fit the ever increasing and newly discovered facts. But here is an ancient book that is ever modern, and one with which all the research of true science and the accumulated discoveries of eighteen centuries are in perfect accord.

There is no other book comparable to the Bible as far as its origin, history, preservation, and the harmony of its various portions, are concerned. This striking unity of its component parts constitutes one of the strongest proofs that the Bible is divinely inspired.

Let us suppose that a number of men from different states were each to bring a block of marble, varying in size and shape, each block bearing a definite number. And let us suppose that after these blocks were assembled according to their respective numbers, a perfectly chiseled statue of Abraham Lincoln were to stand before us. How were these men, who had no contact with one another, able so to hew their blocks of stone to the perfect likeness of Abraham Lincoln? The explanation is simple: *one mind* planned it all, made the patterns, gave the directions, distributed the blocks, and each workman carefully followed the instructions, and a perfect similitude of Lincoln was the result.

In the same manner the various books of the Bible were written by its various authors under the inspiration of *one mind,* and that mind was God.

*   *   *

How hard and dismal this world of ours would be were it not for the Bible! A Bible-less world might never have known of ours were it not for the "Golden Rule" of the "Sermon of the Mount," already given in the third book of the Bible: "Thou shalt love thy neighbor as thyself" (Leviticus 19:18).

When these divine principles were transcribed by the prophets of old, the surrounding heathen world recognized but one law — the law of brute force. Were we to compare the Bible statutes with the laws of ancient Babylon, Assyria, and Egypt, or even with some of the laws of modern times, we would discover a startling and striking difference. The law of Moses knew nothing of the tortures practiced by the Romans, nor did that law permit the equally cruel and horrible inflictions which have abounded in even so-called cultured lands up to the present century.

The principles inculcated by the Bible are most salutary. Such ideals as the Fatherhood of God and the brotherhood of man, wherever believed and practiced, had their origin in the Bible teaching of many centuries ago. Racial hatred was outlawed by God who says in Deuternomy 10:19: "Love ye therefore the stranger: for ye were strangers in the land of Egypt." And again through the prophet Isaiah God says: "for mine house shall be called an house of prayer for all people" (Isaiah 56:7). In Malachi 2:10 we are asked: "Have we not all one Father?"

The law of God, or the moral law, form the background for all modern jurisprudence. The stability of our society, the sanctity of the marriage relation, the principles of civil and religious liberty, respect for the individual conscience in matters of religion, the self-evident truth that God has made all men equal, and has endowed them with certain inalienable rights, among which are life, liberty, and the pursuit of happiness — all have their source in, and spring from, the teachings of Moses and the prophets.

Wherever acts of mercy and deeds of disinterested benevolence are performed to succor the underprivileged and the poor, there you may be sure that the Bible has gone before. The Bible has inspired men to erect hospitals to minister to the sick, to found orphanages for the housing of the fatherless and lost, and to establish homes for the aged in every country and clime. The Bible has elevated womanhood to her rightful place, to be man's "help meet," his equal, to be treated with love, and respect.

The statutes and laws which God gave recognized the dignity of men and regarded human life as sacred. These laws were designed to protect and aid the poor and underprivileged.

1. What other book ever had laws requiring that the wages of the workman should be paid, not quarterly, monthly, or weekly, but before sunset every night? (See Deuteronomy 24:15.)

2. What other book ever forbade the taking of a pledge from a widow for her indebtedness, or required a pawned garment to be returned to a poor man at night? (See Deuteronomy 24:12, 13.)

3. What other book ever had a law allowing the poor or the traveler to eat and fill their hands with fruit from any vineyard or orchard through which they passed, only forbidding their taking any vessels or bags with them to carry fruit away? (See Deuteronomy 23:24, 25.)

4. What other book had a law forbidding men to curse the deaf, or put a stumblingblock in the path of the blind? (See Leviticus 19:14.)

5. What other book had a law which gave every man an inheritance of land, and so secured it that even the king on his throne could not take it from him? It was so arranged that if he himself were compelled to part with his land, he could not sell it outright, but could redeem it at any time when able; and if not, at the end of the jubilee period his children could go and claim their ancient inheritance. (See Leviticus 25:23, 25, 10, 13; also I Kings 21:1-3.)

6. What other book had a law forbidding the husbandman to reap the corners of the fields, or gather the gleanings of his harvest or the fallen grapes of his vineyard, but commanding him to leave them for the poor and the stranger? (See Leviticus 19:9, 10.)

7. What other book had a law which forbade the muzzling of the ox as he was treading out the corn, or which protected the birds upon their nests, and commanded men to show kindness to beasts in distress, even though they belonged to their enemies? (See Deuteronomy 25:4; 22:6, 7; Exodus 23:4, 5.)

8. What other book had a law which required men to love their neighbors as themselves, forbade them to cherish grudges against them, and prohibited malice, tale-bearing, revenge? (See Leviticus 19:16, 18.)

*　　*　　*

God's moral law is still of incalculable blessing to the world.

Have you ever traveled by automobile through unfamiliar country? If so, you considered a road map to be absolutely indispensable.

The Holy Scriptures are just that. They are God's divine road map which is designed to lead us safely through life's uneven, and unfamiliar journey. They point out to us the only road that leads to the kingdom of God and to eternal life. "Thy word is a lamp unto my feet, and is light unto my path" (Psalm 119:105).

The Bible is the only book from among the countless millions of volumes that flood the world, which is effecting such marvelous transformations in the characters and lives of men and women, that even the unbelieving and the agnostic, the skeptics and the infidels cannot deny or gainsay it. Incidentally, whether they know it or not, the irreligious and godless themselves indirectly benefit from the salutary change which the Bible has wrought in the lives of their fellowmen.

A vessel was once wrecked on one of the South Sea Islands. One of the survivors, a godless sailor, realizing that they had been washed ashore on one of the cannibal islands, felt that there was no hope, no way of escape for himself, or the rest of the crew. He stealthily climbed to a hilltop to do a little reconnoitering. Soon his shipmates saw him swinging his arms in wild excitement. Upon inquiry they learned that he had seen a *house of worship*. This took all fear of cannibalism out of his soul. He knew that that house of worship made his neck safe on that cannibal island.

A young infidel recently was traveling in the West with his aunt and uncle who was a banker. They were forced to stop for a night in a rough wayside inn. Feeling somewhat anxious for their safety, they agreed that the young man should sit up and watch, pistol in hand, until midnight, after which time the uncle was to take up the vigil until morning.

There were only two rooms in the cabin. The young friend peeped through a crack in the wall, and saw their host, a rough-looking elderly man, in a mackinaw coat, reach up to a shelf and take down a book. It was the Bible. After he had read it a while he knelt down to pray. This young infidel then calmly began to undress for bed. His uncle was greatly surprised and said, "I thought you were to stay up and watch." But the young man knew only too well that there was no need of sitting up, pistol in hand, to watch all night long in a cabin that was hallowed by the word of God and sanctified by prayer. Wherever the Holy Scriptures exert their influence, there human life is safe.

To deviate in the least from the path of life mapped out for us, might mean our eternal loss. Only in charting our course in harmony with the Scriptures can we be safe. Any philosophy of life or system of ethics, however attractive and inviting its teachings, unless based upon and in perfect accord with God's unerring book, will, in the end, spell eternal ruin.

*   *   *

One of the strongest proofs of the divine authorship of the Bible is its ability to satisfy the highest aspirations and deepest longings of the human heart. In times of distress and sorrow, when waves of despair sweep over our lives, when we need comfort and solace, when in the darkness we grope for the hand of God, then it is that we flee to the Book for encouragement and consolation. When life's burdens oppress us, when sorrow would swallow us up, when the grim reaper lays a loved one in the grave, when we come to the valley of the shadow of death, then we ask for the Bible. And we do not ask in vain, for there is no anxiety that harasses the soul, no problem or frustration which the true child of God is called upon to face, for which God has not made ample and full provision in the Scripture.

When things look blue, read Isaiah chapter 40.

When discouraged, read the 23rd Psalm.

When you are facing a crisis, read Psalm 46.

When you are lonely and fearful, ponder Psalm 27 and 56.

If you are sick, read Psalm 91 and 103.

When you are tempted to do wrong, read Psalm 139.

When you have sinned, read Isaiah 1:18.

When you are bereaved, read Ezekiel 37.

Whoever you are, regardless of how great your difficulty, trouble, sorrow, or bereavement, somewhere in the pages of God's Holy Book is the very help you need.

Every chapter and every verse of the Bible is a direct communication from God to you. It will lead God's people, as the Israelites were led, by the pillar of cloud by day, and the pillar of fire by night.

So search the Scriptures, "Let them not depart from thine eyes; keep them in the midst of thine heart. For they are life unto those that find them, and health [medicine], to all their flesh" (Proverbs 4:21, 22).

Can a book filled with such unsurpassing wisdom be the product of man's unaided intellect? It is said that when Columbus saw the river Orinoco, some one whispered to him that he had discovered an *island*. "Not so," said Columbus. "That mighty torrent must drain the waters of a continent!" Even so, the Book of books, the Bible, does not come from the puny, inferior mind of finite man, but springs from the eternal depths of divine wisdom. It is the expression of the divine plan, the transcript of the divine character. It is the revelation of God!

The early Hebrew nation could well take justifiable pride in this exhaustless treasure which God entrusted to them wherewith to enrich, ennoble, uplift, and bless all the nations of earth for centuries. Yet unborn man, however cultured, is not truly educated unless he has a thorough knowledge of the Bible. To live on and on a stranger to this fountain of life, is to live in name only.

God knows the wants of the soul. Pomp, riches, honor, and temporal security cannot satisfy the heart. "Incline your ear, and come unto me: hear, and your soul shall live," says the Scripture in Isaiah 55:3. The rich, the poor, the high, the low, are alike welcome. God promises to relieve the burdened mind, to comfort the sorrowing heart, and to give hope to the despondent soul. Many are seeking to satisfy their restless longing with the things of the world and with the praise and approbation of men; but when all that is gained, they find that they have toiled only to secure a broken reservoir from which they cannot quench their thirst. To all these the invitation is extended:

"Ho, every one that thirsteth, come ye to the waters, and he that hath no money; come ye, buy, and eat; yea, come buy wine and milk without money and without price. Wherefore do ye spend money for that which is not bread? and your labor for that which satisfieth not? hearken diligently unto me, and eat ye that which is good, and let your soul delight itself in fatness" (Isaiah 55:1, 2).

The following story is told about a widow who owned a few acres of parched land in one of the western states. Her property was considered of but little value, and barely produced enough for her sustenance. One day geological experts were investigating various soils in the vicinity of this farm, and chanced to analyze a part of the ground owned by this widow. To their surprise they discovered that it contained oil. The entire acreage of her farm was then investigated, and it was found that beneath that barren land trodden by the widow's feet for many years, lay immense stores of oil, worth thousands of dollars. This family had lived in poverty while riches were within their reach.

A vastly greater treasure has been in possession of the civilized race for three thousand years and more. That priceless treasure is the Holy Scriptures. These sacred writings have frequently been trodden under foot as it were; their soul-stirring messages have often been unappreciated and even ignored. Thus it has been for centuries, until scholars, who thirsted for truth and righteousness, investigated the writings of the prophets and discovered in them the treasures of wisdom and knowledge.

Shall not we, who are the children of our creator and joint heirs with Jesus, cherish and obey the heavenly light and truth which emanate from Bible writings, and satisfy our heart's desires by drinking deeply and freely of this life-giving current? As the depth of Bible wisdom and knowledge is impressed upon our mind and heart, may we, too, pray as did David of old: "Open thou mine eyes, that I may behold wondrous things out of thy law!" (Psalm 119:18).

11

Accuracy of the Scriptures

11

ACCURACY OF THE SCRIPTURES

The Bible abounds in statements of a historical, anthropological, geological, archaeological, and astronomical nature. If but one of its statements could be proved false from a historical or scientific point of view, if only one essential error were discovered, it would arouse uncertainty and cast theological doubt upon the entire volume of Scripture. The Scripture's claim to divine inspiration would then have to be abandoned and forsaken, for a single vital inaccuracy would be sufficient to remove the Scriptures from their exalted pedestal of infallibility, and place them on a level with the common productions of erring, finite men.

For many ages, agnostics, skeptics, and infidels have wearied themselves in their fruitless effort to discover just such an error. Armed with pseudo-scientific instruments, and with a zeal worthy of a better cause, time and again these men have claimed to have exploded what they were pleased to call the "myth of the infallibility of the Bible." But have any of their "proofs" of so-called Bible inaccuracies survived the test of time? Not one! Subsequent discoveries have not only served to dissipate these "proofs" into thin air, but have wholly and entirely vindicated the Scriptures—if indeed they needed such vindication in the first place.

*   *   *

Perhaps no other scriptural fact has been subjected to more criticism by the skeptics than has the Bible record of a universal flood. A detailed description of the flood is given in Genesis 6-9. In the past, this record has not only been questioned, but ridiculed as well. But time has brought about a change. Years ago, a treatise

127

appeared in a popular science book, entitled, *Science Explains the Great Flood,* in which the following statement was made: "The flood conditions which science now knows, actually occurred in historic times." And indeed we have world-wide evidence today, testifying to the truthfulness of the Bible story.

In the folklore of all the great races of mankind there are traditions of the Flood that have been handed down from generation to generation. There are also so-called "Deluge tablets" that give many accounts of a universal flood which closely resemble the description given us in the Bible. These tablets were written by *different* people in *different* places, and at *different* times. Several accounts of the deluge are found in India. In Roman legendary history we learn that Ovid, the Roman poet, in the first century B.C. gave a vivid description of the flood. But it is in China where some of the Flood proofs are found. (See *Discourses on China; Asiatic Researches,* Vol. 2, p. 376, by Sir William Jones.) In the New World, the Eskimos, the Alaska Indians, and other North American tribes have similar traditions of a universal flood, indicating not only a common source, but an actual occurrence.

High shore lines above the present water level are found on most seacoasts. There are also clearly marked old shore lines high on the mountain sides around interior basins with shrunken lakes, showing where these lakes once stood. All the rivers of the world, whether small or large, have similar terraces or stairlike benches.

One of the pet theories advanced by the critics was, that there is not enough water on this earth to cover the entire surface of our planet. Modern scientific research, however, after careful mathematical calculations, declares that if all the present inequalities of the globe were leveled out, so that all the solid part of the earth's surface were a uniform plain, the globe would be completely covered by water to a depth of nearly 9,000 feet, or more than one and a half miles.

Some skeptics have doubted whether Noah's ark was sufficiently sea-worthy to survive the maelstrom of the flood. Now it is a matter of history that the renowned old Navy battleship "U.S.S. Oregon," was built on the exact dimensions of Noah's ark, only one-seventh smaller in scale. This ship has proved so seaworthy, that according to the *Pittsburgh Press* of April 20, 1944, although it was once relegated to the nation's scrap pile due to its age, it was again taken back "to Portland, Oregon, a proud vessel about to take an active part in the (Second World) war." To date she is evidently unsinkable! She served us well in the South Pacific and in the Philippine campaign.

The existence of immense bone beds in different parts of the world also prove that there was a universal deluge. There is a mountain in Europe, called "the mountain of bones," because it is covered with bones all the way from the base to the summit with thirty-five different kinds of animal remains, all indicating that these animals perished at the same time. Indeed the Flood is the only satisfactory explanation of the vast coal beds and oil fields, as well as of the antiquated remains of men, animals, reptiles, birds, trees, and plants, which are buried in all parts of the world, and of the sea shells that are found on the tops of high mountains in different places of the world. The Smithsonian Institute can give ample proof of such conditions and discoveries.

Sir Henry Howorty, speaking of the huge mammoths found in Siberia, says: "They were in full health with their stomachs distended with indigested food." Scientists tell us that the heads of those frozen mammoths indicated a clear case of drowning. Fossil fish are found buried in compact form many feet thick in the coal beds, in oil sands, and great layers of rock, many of them with their fins extended as when living. J. M. MacFarlane in his book, *Fishes, the Source of Petroleum,* says that a large proportion of the petroleum in the world is derived from fossil fish. Chemical analysis corroborates this when it tells us that this oil is either of animal or vegetable origin, or a combination of both.

In the *Geological Magazine,* Vol. 12, p. 531, a scientist speaking of the animal and vegetable fossil remains found in the polar regions, says that they all alike testify that at one time a warm climate prevailed over the entire world. Dr. H. H. Neuville agrees with this, saying that the extinct mammoths buried in the frozen earth of Northern Siberia are as tropical or subtropical as the elephants of today. (See the Smithsonian Report of 1919, page 332.) The same kinds of tropical plants found in the stomachs of the frozen animals, occur in abundance in the frozen muds, and in the shale and great coal beds, indicating that a great, and sudden climatic change overtook these monsters and engulfed them, as they wandered over their feeding grounds. The ice became a natural refrigerator that preserved their flesh for centuries.

Another evidence of a universal Deluge is presented by the vast coal beds in many parts of the earth's crust. Geologists now admit that these coal beds are the petrified and consolidated masses of vast forests of antiquity buried by some great natural catastrophe.

Very often the remains of trees which grew in very different habitats are indiscriminately mixed in the coal seams below the earth's light. As they could never have become associated together under normal conditions, they obviously must have been thrown together under extremely abnormal circumstances. Moreover, the marvelous impressions of leaves and the markings on the trunks of trees, which are often found in the coal deposits, clearly indicate sudden rather than gradual burial, for these impressions could only have been produced before the vegetation had time to decay.

To sum it all up—the only monument we have today of pre-Flood days is the wreckage of a corrupt world, whose submerged tropical trees and animals in the perpetual snow and ice of the far north, and its myriads of sea creatures buried in the sands and rocks of very land, have through the ages left us irrefutable evidence of the Bible record of the Flood.

*   *   *

Critics of the Scriptures used to challenge the historicity of persons and places. For example, it was alleged by these skeptics that the Hittite nation mentioned in Scripture was a myth, that the story of Israel in Egypt was an invention, that Moses was not the real author of the Pentateuch inasmuch as the art of writing was not known until long after the time of Moses; that Belshazzar of the book of Daniel was a fictitious character, etc., etc. Ponderous volumes were written to sustain these views, and may still be found in some libraries.

Have these criticisms and the "evidences" to support them, survived the test of time? No, not one. Through the many long centuries and even milleniums, the Lord God has preserved a veritable arsenal of facts for these last days, in order to confirm the historic and scientific declarations of Scripture. Every time the spade of the archaeologist is upturned, the accuracy of Bible statements is established. Thanks to the modern science of archaeology, the ancient stones "are crying out" in mute but powerful testimony to the reliability of Biblical history.

In the British Museum are exhibited the famous Tel-el-Amarna tablets discovered in Tel-el-Amarna, Egypt. The writing upon these tablets is in cuneiform characters, and was written *one hundred years before Moses' time.* In the same magnificent museum is also exhibited copy of the famous black stone of Susa. This stone was discovered by M. de Morgan in December, 1901, and upon it are inscribed laws of Hammurabi (believed to be identical with Amraphel, king of Babylon, as mentioned in Genesis) *who lived five hundred years before Moses,* and was doubtless a contemporary of Abraham. "The Babylonia of the age of Abraham," says the archaeologist Sayce, "was a more highly educated country than the England of George the Third." Inasmuch then as Moses lived several centuries *after* Abraham, how ridiculous now appear the assertions of the critics that Moses could not have written the Pentateuch, because writing had not as yet been invented in his day:

In the list of kings compiled by the Greek historians, Nabonidus was designated as the last king of Babylonia. Inasmuch as the fifth chapter of the book of Daniel state that Belshazzar was the last king of that empire, the critics declared the Bible false, and Belshazzar a fictitious character. Today, however, we have more than five hundred ancient tablets proving that Belshazzar was co-ruler with his aged father, Nabonidus, whose seat of government was at Tema in Arabia, while that of Belshazzar was in Babylon.

As for the story of Israel in Egypt, which the skeptics ridiculed for so long, it, too, has been fully confirmed by scientific discoveries. The Bible record informs us that:

"they [the children of Israel] built for Pharaoh treasure cities, Pithom and Raamses. . . . And the Egyptians made the children of Israel to serve with rigor: And they made their lives bitter with hard bondage, *in mortar, and in brick,* and in all manner of service. . . wherein they made them serve, was with rigor" (Exodus 1:11, 13, 14).

"And Pharaoh commanded the same day the taskmasters of the people, and their officers, saying, Ye shall *no more give the people straw* to make bricks, as heretofore: let them go and gather straw for themselves. . . . So the people were scattered abroad throughout all the land of Egypt to gather stubble instead of straw. And the taskmasters hasted them, saying, Fulfil your works, your daily tasks, as when there was straw" (Exodus 5:6, 7, 12, 13).

Note the striking similarity between the Bible narrative and the following nineteenth century archaeological discoveries:

In 1883, Edouard Naville, Egyptologist of the University of Geneva, Switzerland, discovered and identified this store city of Pithom mentioned in this Scripture. He tells us that it was built by Ramses II for storehouse purposes. Dr. Naville declared that "the store chambers themselves have now been uncovered. They were very strongly constructed, and divided by brick partitions from eight to ten feet thick, the bricks being sun-baked, and made, some with and some without straw."

Melvin G. Kyle, archaeologist, went to the site of Dr. Naville's discovery, in order to investigate the findings for himself, and this is what he wrote: "Every point in the story of the insurrection is written upon the ruins of Pithom. The place was called Pithom; it was a store city; the bricks were laid in 'mortor,' contrary to the usual Egyptian method of brickwork; the bricks in the lower courses were filled with good clean straw, those of the middle courses were made with stubble mixed with weeds and all pulled by the roots, while the bricks of the upper courses were made of Nile mud without the mixture of any building material whatever; and all these things were found in the ancient region of Succoth as the Bible asserts" (J. S. Griffiths, *Exodus in the Light of Archaeology* pages 44, 45).

Jericho was the first city of Palestine to fall before the Hebrew invaders. The ruins of the ancient city were uncovered between 1930 and 1933, by the Marston Archaeological Expedition, under the direction of Professor John Garstang, noted English archaeologist. The excavator sums up his discoveries thus: "Set side by side with the Biblical narrative, every essential detail the record of the capture and destruction of Jericho by the Israelites under Joshua seem plausible" (*New Bible Evidence*, page 234).

In Joshua 2:5 we read, "And it came to pass about the time of shutting of *the gate....*" This Scripture would indicate that the city had but *one gate,* which fact is corroborated by excavations. In Joshua 2:15 we read that Rahab's "house was upon the town wall, and she dwelt upon the wall." The excavations show that Jericho was surrounded by two walls, fifteen feet apart, and that houses were built on top of these walls binding them together.

Many other equally striking discoveries that substantiate the Scriptures might be cited here if space permitted. W. H. Main, in his book, *Our Bible in the Light of Modern Discovery,* says: "The veracity and authenticity of that old Book, suspected and challenged, stand unimpeached before the testimony of nations hostile to Israel. These ancient words [or inscriptions] chiseled in everlasting rocks, echoing down through forty centuries of time, set their seal of approval on the truth of the Holy Scriptures. With Egypt on the Southwest, Assyria and Babylon on the east, Phoenicia and the Hittites on the north, we have a solid square of unimpeachable, and everincreasing testimony to the veracity and authenticity of the books of the Old Testament."

Furthermore, in the thirty-eighth chapter of the book of Job, written more than three thousand years ago, we find the Lord asking Job some hard questions on the mysteries of nature. Many of these questions seemed strange until modern science discovered their true meaning.

One of these questions is: "Hast thou entered into the *springs of the sea?* or hast thou walked in the search of the depth?" (Job 38:16). The existence of "springs" or well-defined streams or currents in the oceans was not known until the seas began to be navigated, long after Columbus discovered America. It was Benjamin Franklin in 1770 who made the first chart of what he called the Gulf Stream. He secured his information from a Nantucket whaling captain, who told him that no whales were found in these *streams* of the sea. His knowledge, of course, was limited. These ocean rivers as we now know them, such as the Gulf Stream, the Brazil Current, the Labrador Current, the Japan Current, the Equatorial Current, and others, keep the waters of the seven seas in circulation, and also greatly affect the climate of all the lands that they touch. It took man three thousand years to learn that which the Scripture so simply stated three millenniums before.

The second half of the above question, "hast thou walked in the search of the depth?" undoubtedly refers to the great depths of the oceans, which in some places are now known to be 35,400 feet, or almost seven miles. This makes the depth of the sea greater than the height of the land, for the highest mountain is only 29,141 feet above sea level.

Almost three thousand years ago the Scripture stated: "The wind goeth toward the south, and turneth about unto the north; it whirleth about continually, and the wind returneth again according to his circuits" (Ecclesiastes 1:6).

It was not until centuries after these words of Scripture were written that it was discovered that the winds travel in circuits and according to fixed and unchangeable laws. They are so regular in their movements that scientists are able to forecast atmospheric changes long in advance of the arrival of a storm. There is no stagnant air in the atmospheric heavens, for there are the trade winds traveling from the northeast in the Northern Hemisphere, and from the southeast in the Southern Hemisphere, the anti-trades whose course is in the opposite direction.

It is now well-known that water is continually leaving the sea through evaporation, and is carried by the clouds and poured out in rain to serve vegetation. By means of the streams and rivers it flows back again to the sea from whence it originally came. This scientific fact was stated several millenniums ago in Scripture. We quote Ecclesiastes 1:7 and also Amos 5:8: "All the rivers run into the sea; yet the sea is not full; unto the place from whence the rivers come, thither they return again" (Ecclesiastes 1:7). "Seek Him... that calleth for the waters of the sea, and poureth them out upon the face of the earth" (Amos 5:8).

Can we of this enlightened age give credence to the story of Jonah and the whale? The Bible states that "the Lord had prepared a great fish to swallow up Jonah. And Jonah was in the belly of the fish three days and three nights....And the Lord spake unto the fish, and it vomited out Jonah upon the dry land" (Jonah 1:17; 2:10).

Long have skeptics ridiculed this story, until similar experiences of modern Jonahs silenced these Bible critics forever. In February 1891, the *Literary Digest* printed the story of James Bartley, a sailor, who was actually swallowed by a whale, that had been harpooned and wounded to death. Bartley lived to tell the story. We quote a short excerpt of the narrative: "When the monster had ceased moving...the work of cutting it up began....When it was ended, the stomach of the whale was opened. What was the surprise of the whalemen to find in it their lost comrade, James Bartley, unconscious but *alive*." It was some time before he completely recovered from his terrible ordeal. This experience is by no means an isolated one. However, those who accept the Bible as infallible need no proof beyond its own claim. The Psalmist says concerning God's Word, "his truth endureth to all generations" (Psalm 100:5).

*   *   *

From the foregoing facts we see that the Holy Scriptures, though penned milleniums before the first glimmer of the age of science, are singularly uncorrupted by the fables, superstitions, and ignorance, that universally prevailed at the time of their writing. We have learned that time and research are the Bible's greatest corroborators, and that it stands the acid test of investigation. It speaks with authority, for it is Truth, and truth needs no other defense than that it is the truth.

> The Bible stands like a rock undaunted
> Mid the raging storm of time:
> Its pages burn with the truth eternal,
> And they glow with a light sublime.

The story is told of a Christian mother who on her deathbed gave her wayward son her most cherished possession—a Bible. She assured him that God's book contained hidden treasure, and counseled him to read its sacred pages. Not being interested in spiritual things, the young man laid the book aside until many years later, when sickness, sorrow, and poverty overtook him. Then it was that he thought of his dying mother's request. As he opened the sacred volume, he found, to his great astonishment, that his mother had placed a number of thousand dollar bills among its pages! Not only was the young man enriched materially, but as he read, he discovered the infinitely greater riches, the imperishable treasures of the unsearchable wisdom and knowledge found in God's word. With David he could say: "The judgments of the Lord are true and righteous altogether....More to be desired are they than gold, yea, than much fine gold....and in keeping of them there is great reward" (Psalms 19:1-11).

Why need anyone go through life impoverished when such untold riches are ever at hand? Shall we not gratefully accept the Book of books as the divine and infallible guide toward our heavenly home?

12

The Calling of Israel

THE CALLING OF ISRAEL

The existence and preservation of the Hebrew people constitutes one of history's strangest phenomena. Many ancient nations, some of whom were numerically greater and politically more powerful than the Hebraic nation, have long since ceased to exist. The Hittites, the Amorites, the Canaanites, the Philistines, the Moabites, the Babylonians, and an army of other equally powerful nations of antiquity, have all passed away, and have not left a single inhabitant or transient to perpetuate their name. But the Hebrew nation survives, notwitstanding the inhuman, merciless, and pitiless persecutions which it has endured throughout the ages. This singular fact has evoked the following comment by the historian Milman: "Massacred by the thousands, yet springing up again from their undying stock, the Jews appear at all times and in all regions. Their perpetuity, their national immortality, is at once the most curious problem to the political inquirer, to the religious man a subject of profound and awful admiration" (*History of the Jew*, Vol. 2, p. 299).

What is the cause of Israel's miraculous preservation? How shall we explain this historical enigma? Is it due to chance, or coincidence, that the physical offspring of Abraham's seed, the present day Jews, continue to exist, or is it rather because of God's merciful and overruling providence? The prophet Jeremiah expresses it thus: "It is of the Lord's mercies that we are not consumed, because his compassions fail not" (Lamentations 3:22).

Yes, it is God who has decreed that this very nation shall continue as long as time itself shall last, and that it shall never be utterly consumed. Note carefully the following divine pronouncements concerning Israel, as recorded by the ancient seers: "And yet for all that, when they be in the land of their enemies, I will not cast them away, neither will I...destroy them utterly...for I am the Lord their God" (Leviticus 26:44). And again: "For I will make a full end of all the nations whither I have driven thee: *but I will not make a full end of thee*" (Jeremiah 46:28).

*   *   *

You ask: Why did God accord such extraordinary favors to Israel? It is because He has an extraordinary work for them to do, a work which is to be of inestimable benefit to the entire human race both specifically and in general.

God furnished Israel with every facility for becoming the greatest nation on the earth. It was God's purpose that by the revelation of His character through Israel, men should be drawn to His Son. This began with the call of Abraham.

After the flood, idolatry became well-nigh universal. The vast majority of earth's inhabitants had willfully and deliberately rejected the dominion of the living God, and set aside His grace and holy judgments. The black night of heathenism, accompanied by its degrading and demoralizing systems of worship, had spread its influence far and wide until it had enveloped the entire then known world.

But the true faith was not to become extinct. Abraham who dwelt in Ur of the Chaldees, refused to render obeisance to idols. Faithful among the faithless, uncorrupted by the prevailing heathenism Abraham steadfastly adhered to the worship of the one true God. His father and near of kin, however, were idolaters. Abraham's environment and home influences were not conducive to spirituality. In order that God might qualify him for his great work of preserving the worship of the true God in the earth, the following call came to Abraham:

"Now the Lord had said unto Abram, Get thee out of thy country, and from thy kindred, and from thy father's house, unto a land that I will show thee: and I will make of thee a great nation, and I will bless thee, and make thy name great; and thou shalt be a blessing: And I will bless them that bless thee, and curse him that curseth thee: and in thee shall all families of the earth be blessed. So Abram departed, as the Lord had spoken unto him (Genesis 12:1-4). This is theologically referred to as the Abrahamic Covenant.

It was no small sacrifice that God required of Abraham. Strong ties bound him to his home, his kindred, and his country. Nevertheless, he did not hesitate to renounce his father's idolatrous worship, since it was incompatible with the worship of the true living God. Abraham did not plead that his fathers' religion was good enough for him. He chose to make God the ultimate in his affections; and how far-reaching was the influence of that choice! But for Abraham's courageous stand, idolatry with its revolting and licentious rites of devil worship might well have become universal.

Many of earth's children today are tested as was Abraham. While God does not speak to them directly, He speaks to them through the teachings of the Scriptures and by the Holy Spirit.

In Joshua 24:2 we read: "And Joshua said unto all the people, Thus saith the Lord God of Israel, Your fathers dwelt on the other side of the flood in old time, even Terah, the father of Abraham, and the father of Nachor: and they served other gods."

In order to reach Canaan, Abraham had to cross the river Euphrates, and that is the reason the Canaanites called him "the Hebrew," which comes from the word *ai-ver,* meaning "on the other side." This is where Abraham became the father of the Hebrew nation, and his posterity were called "Hebrews" in order to differentiate between them from the races who dwelt east of the Euphrates.

* * *

The Lord did not bestow special favors upon Israel because they were numerically superior to other nations. We quote: "The Lord did not set his love upon you, nor choose you, because ye were more in number than any people; for *ye were the fewest of all people"* (Deuteronomy 7:7).

Neither was Israel designed to be just another political entity. Their exaltation as a nation was on religious, and *not* on political grounds. Their prosperity, and their very existence as a nation, was contingent upon their faithfulness in fulfilling their divinely appointed task. They were told:

"For thou art a holy people unto the Lord thy God: The Lord thy God hath chosen thee to be a special people unto himself, above all people that are upon the face of the earth" (Deuteronomy 7:6). "Now therefore, if ye will obey my voice indeed, and keep my covenant, then ye shall be a peculiar treasure unto me above all people:...And ye shall be unto me a kingdom of priests, and a holy nation" (Exodus 19:5, 6).

Israel's mission was a universal one. They were never to become narrow or self-centered. From them the light of God's truth concerning the Messiah was to radiate to the gentile nations about them, who were steeped in the night of ignorance and superstition.

"Behold, I have taught you statutes and judgments, even as the Lord my God commanded me, that ye should do so in the land whither ye go to possess it. Keep therefore and do them; for this is your wisdom and your understanding *in the sight of the nations, which shall hear all these statutes,* and say, Surely this great nation is a wise and understanding people. For what nation is there so great, who hath God so nigh unto them, as the Lord our God is in all things that we call upon him for? And what nation is there so great, that hath statutes and judgments so righteous as all this law, which I set before you this day?" (Deuteronomy 4:5-8).

*   *   *

God called Abraham to be the father of the faithful, and his life was to stand forever as an example of faith to succeeding generations. But few realize the full import, and the vast implications of these promises of God to Abraham; namely, that in him and *in his seed* all the families of the earth were to be blessed! Because of man's departure from holiness, the curse of sin, with its attendant and endless train of woe and evil, rested heavily upon the human race. Through Abraham, however, and through his seed, this course was somehow to be lifted. Mankind was to be given an opportunity to escape the thraldom and slavery of sin, and again to enjoy the blessedness of communion and of perfect harmony with its Maker.

All the families of the earth were to be blessed in Abraham's seed. Whom did God have in mind by the "seed" of Abraham? The first promise of a "seed" is recorded in Genesis 3:15, and it was made to Adam and Eve in the garden of Eden, after they had yielded to the subtle insinuations of Satan, and had joined with him in revolt against God and His sacred Word. God declared that the "seed of the woman" was to bruise or crush the serpent's (or Satan's) head.

The Holy Scriptures interpret this "seed" to be the Messiah— the Redeemer, the Holy One of Israel. When God made the promise to Abraham—"in thy seed shall all the nations of the earth be blessed"—He did not say "thy seeds," in the plural, but "thy seed," in the singular. Why did God use the singular noun? The answer is found in the Scriptures, which inform us that this "seed" refers to the one and only Saviour, through whom the blessing which God pronounced upon Abraham might come upon all the nations.

*   *   *

The children of Israel were pre-eminently the Messianic people. It was in that sense that they were to bless and benefit all the nations. The impressive and symbolic ritual given to Israel was designed to attract disciples from every nation, and to arouse their inquiries as to the significance of the services they beheld, services that foreshadowed the coming Saviour, the Deliverer. Thus the cheering message of a Saviour to come, was to echo and re-echo to the ends of the earth.

However, the Messiah was not to be an exclusive gift to the Jews. In the words of the prophet Isaiah: "It is a light thing that thou [Saviour] shouldest be my servant to raise up the tribes of Jacob, and to restore the preserved of Israel: I will also give thee *for a light to the Gentiles, that thou mayest be my salvation unto the end of the earth*" (Isaiah 49:6).

The very geographical location of Palestine bore eloquent witness to the universal mission of the Jews. "Thus saith the Lord God; This is Jerusalem: I have set it *in the midst of the nations*" (Ezekiel 5:5). God placed His chosen people in the Holy Land because it was strategically situated in the center and crossroads of the world. It is the hub from which the spokes radiate to the teeming multitudes of Europe, Asia, Africa and the new world.

If we need any further evidence of the Messianic mission of the Hebrews then let us try to discover a reason for the determined and fixed purpose of the heathen nations utterly to destroy and annihilate the children of Israel. Why were the Moabites, the Amorites, the Amalekites, and other nations too numerous to mention, so bent on blotting out the name and remembrance of Israel from under heaven? What sinister power moved these nations to hate Israel with such unyielding and bitter hatred? Why should such deep and malignant enmity have existed between them and the surrounding nations? The underlying reasons may be traced to the following causes.

When the promise of a Deliverer was first made by God in the garden of Eden, the Lord had declared that enmity would exist between the seed of the woman and the seed of the serpent, or the devil. Satan understood from this divine declaration that his work of depraving human nature was to be interrupted; that by some means, man was to be given power to resist him. As the plan of salvation was progressively unfolded, Satan learned that God had not abandoned the human race to his control, but that a Deliverer— the Saviour—would challenge his (Satan's) supremacy, break his power, and finally overcome him, or as the Scripture declares—

"bruise his head" (Genesis 3:15). When Satan learned from the pronouncements that this Messiah was to come from the tribe of Judah, or the Hebrews, his rage against this nation knew no bounds. He determined to frustrate God's purpose for Israel, and he conceived a plan which he believed would blot out this Messianic people from the face of the earth. By this diabolical scheme Satan hoped to prevent the coming of the Deliverer.

It was Satan who moved the nations of antiquity, the Amalekites, the Midianites, the Philistines, the Amorites, etc., to wage wars of extermination and annihilation against the Messianic people. It was he who fired them with an insane zeal to destroy Israel. These heathen nations were Satan's willing subject; they had chosen his rule, obeyed his commands. Having rejected the supremacy and authority of the God of the universe, they could not tolerate His people. God, however, intervened to frustrate their murderous designs. The Lord fought for Israel, so that no weapon formed against them could prosper.

For nearly two thousand years after Abraham left his kindred and his people, God miraculously wrought in behalf of Israel in order to preserve their national existence. Despite their numerous backslidings and digressions from His holy precepts, the Lord bore patiently with them.

*   *   *

Great were the honors, privileges, and favors which God bestowed upon ancient Israel. No other people were ever entrusted with such an exalted mission as was committed to this nation. As a goodly vine God had hedged them about by His guardian care, and nurtured them through His messages of love and entreaty by the mouth of His servants, the prophets. "What could have been done more to my vineyard," He exclaimed, "that I have not done in it?" (See Isaiah 5:1-7.) He digged and pruned this vine of His own planting, and tenderly cherished it, in the hope that it might bring forth fruit.

But with all these honors and privileges came corresponding responsibilities. Israel was to reveal the principles of the kingdom of God in the midst of a fallen and wicked world. Would they remain true to their God-given trust? Would they diligently and prayerfully study the prophetic scrolls, and watch for the coming of the promised One, their Messiah? How would Israel relate itself to the "seed," the Messiah, the Holy One of Israel, through whom God designed to make them a praise in the earth, and in whom all the families of the earth were to be blessed? Mighty issues for the world and for the Hebrew nation were at stake.

Specific and detailed predictions were given to Israel through their several prophets concerning the true Messiah. In the Torah, in the Psalms, and in the writings of the prophets are found scores of Messianic prophecies and statements by which the true Redeemer was to be identified. Has he come, or is his first advent still future?

*   *   *

It is of the utmost importance that we base our answer to this vital Messianic question on scriptural evidence. In His infinite love, God overruled in the affairs of nations and preserved Abraham's offspring so that each one of them might individually make his decision on this momentous issue. Let us, therefore, with them investigate the Scriptures for ourselves, prayerfully studying them with a sincere desire to know the truth and obey it, and we shall receive heaven-sent enlightment. Our temporal as well as our eternal interests depend upon our right relationship to God's written Word.

God has a glorious plan for every child of earth and He has revealed this wondrous plan in the Holy Scriptures. What untold happiness, what boundless joys await all who will search the Scriptures as for hidden treasure! The words of Jehoshaphat, king of Judah, addressed to ancient Israel, apply with equal force to modern people the world over: "Believe in the Lord your God, so shall ye be established; believe his prophets, so shall ye prosper" (II Chronicles 20:20).

Everything depends upon our attitude to God's written Word. If we are to achieve true success and prosperity, we must make the Holy Scriptures our daily companion and counsellor. The following admonition addressed by God to Joshua is equally applicable to all of us: "This book of the law shall not depart out of thy mouth; but thou shalt meditate therein day and night, that thou mayest observe to do according to all that is written therein: for then thou shalt make thy way prosperous, and then thou shalt have good success" (Joshua 1:8).

And the Psalmist declares: "Wherewithal shall a young man cleanse his way? by taking heed thereto according to thy word... Thy word is a lamp unto my feet, and a light unto my path. ...The entrance of thy words giveth light; it giveth understanding unto the simple" (Psalm 119:9, 105, 130).

13

Discussions on Heaven

DISCUSSIONS ON HEAVEN

The mass of people wonder what lies in wait for them beyond death, and there are still millions more who, when they think of death, wish they had never been born. Why is this? It is because they do not know what the Bible teaches concerning life after death. This world is filled with sin, filth, vice, crime, murder, corruption, wickedness, sorrow, heartaches, strife, war, hurricanes, earthquakes, fires, drouth, disease, political intrigue—and death; but in the earth made new the Scripture says: "The wolf also shall dwell with the lamb, and the leopard shall lie down with the kid; and the calf and the young lion and the fatling together; and a little child shall lead them. And the cow and the bear shall feed; their young ones shall lie down together: and the lion shall eat straw like the ox.... They shall not hurt nor destroy in all my holy mountain: for the earth shall be full of the knowledge of the Lord, as the waters cover the sea" (Isaiah 11:6, 7, 9).

"Then the eyes of the blind shall be opened, and the ears of the deaf shall be unstopped. Then shall the lame man leap as a hart, and the tongue of the dumb sing: for in the wilderness shall waters break out, and streams in the desert" (Isaiah 35:5, 6).

Inasmuch as the heaven is so wonderful, we want to know what the Bible teaches concerning it. This old world of sin is to be destroyed and all the wicked with it, and God will create the new heavens and a new earth. Notice these words found in Isaiah 65:17-19; 66:22, 23: "For, behold, I create new heavens and a new earth: and the former shall not be remembered, nor come into mind. But be ye glad and rejoice forever in that which I create: for, behold, I create Jerusalem a rejoicing, and her people a joy. And I will rejoice in Jerusalem, and joy in my people: and the voice

149

of weeping shall be no more heard in her, nor the voice of crying
....For as the new heavens and the new earth, which I will make,
shall remain before me, saith the Lord, so shall your seed and your
name remain. And it shall come to pass, that from one new moon
to another, and from one Sabbath to another, shall all flesh come
to worship before me, saith the Lord."

The Scripture speaks of three heavens: atmospheric, stellar, and
paradisiac.

The atmospheric heaven is the part of heaven where the clouds
form and where the birds fly. It is known as the first heaven. Concerning it we read in Genesis 1:20: "And God said, Let the waters
bring forth abundantly the moving creature that hath life, and
fowl that may fly above the earth in the open firmament of *heaven.*"
And we read further: "When he uttered his voice, there is a multitude of waters in the *heavens,* and he causeth the vapors to ascend
from the ends of the earth; he maketh lightnings with rain, and
bringeth forth the wind out of his treasures" (Jeremiah 10:13).

From the above Scripture it is clear that the place in the firmament where birds fly is called heaven. This is the place where the
atmosphere exists and therefore, this would be the first heaven.

The stellar heaven is that part of the heavens where the sun,
moon, and stars have their being and move in their orbits. It is
known as the second heaven. Notice the words found in Genesis
15:5: "And he brought him forth abroad, and said, Look now
toward *heaven,* and tell the stars, if thou be able to number them."

Now let us read further.

"The heavens declare the glory of God; and the firmament sheweth
his handywork....In them hath he set a tabernacle for the sun"
(Psalm 19:1, 4).

"And God said, Let there be lights in the firmament of *heaven*
to divide the day from the night; and let them be for signs, and for
seasons, and for days, and years. And let them be for lights in the
firmament of the *heaven* to give light upon the earth, and it was so.
And God made two great lights: the greater light to rule the day,
and the lesser light to rule the night: he made the stars also. And
God set them in the firmament of the *heaven* to give light upon
the earth, And to rule over the day and over the night, and to divide
the light from the darkness: and God saw that it was good. And
the evening and the morning were the fourth day" (Genesis 1:14-19).

Here we find that God calls the space where sun, moon, and stars
have their being *heaven.*

Paradise, or what we usually refer to as heaven, is known as the third heaven. We read concerning the third heaven that it is a real place. "Behold, the *heaven* and the *heaven of heavens* is the Lord's thy God, the earth also, with all that therein is" (Deuteronomy 10:14).

Here God calls Paradise the heaven of heavens.

The third heaven, or paradise, is the place where God dwells. Notice these words found in Psalm 102:20: "For he hath looked down from the height of his sanctuary; from heaven did the Lord behold the earth."

Will the saved dead be in heaven? According to the plan of salvation the saved dead are already redeemed from the earth. Notice, the language used in the Bible concerning the saved dead. "I will ransom them from the power of the grave; I will redeem them from death: O death, where are thy plagues? O grave, where is thy destruction: repentance shall be hid from mine eyes" (Hosea 13:14).

Further to show the power of God to deliver the saved dead let us read from Daniel 12:1: "And at that time shall Michael stand up, the great prince which standeth for the children of thy people: and there shall be a time of trouble, such as never was since there was a nation even to that same time: and at that time thy people shall be delivered, every one that shall be found written in the book. And many of them that sleep in the dust of the earth shall awake, some to everlasting life, and some to shame and everlasting contempt."

Here we notice that the saved dead awake to everlasting life but the wicked to everlasting condemnation. Now notice the beautiful words concerning the re-creation of the bodies of the saved as found in Isaiah 35:5, 6:

"Then the eyes of the blind shall be opened, and the ears of the deaf shall be unstopped. Then shall the lame man leap as an hart, and the tongue of the dumb sing: for in the wilderness shall waters break out, and streams in the desert."

"And in that day shall the deaf hear the words of the book, and the eyes of the blind shall see out of obscurity, and out of darkness. The meek also shall increase their joy in the Lord, and the poor among men shall rejoice in the Holy One of Israel" (Isaiah 29:18, 19).

"For I know that my redeemer liveth and that he shall stand at the latter day upon the earth: and after they have thus destroyed my skin, yet from my flesh shall I see God" (Job 19:25, 26).

Here we have read the promise of God that even death cannot prevent the resurrection of a glorious, immortal body, to the glory of God in Christ Jesus.

The day is dawning when God is going to eradicate sin and sinners, and then He will create new heavens and a new earth wherein dwelleth righteousness. The conditions of this old world, that is, this sinful world that we now live in, will pass away.

* * *

Will death ever come again? Some people often wonder. The answer is No, death will never come again. Notice these words found in Isaiah 35:10: "And the ransomed of the Lord shall return, and come to Zion with songs and everlasting joy upon their heads; they shall obtain joy and gladness, and sorrow and sighing shall flee away."

Now notice in this text in Isaiah 25:8, 9: "He will swallow up death in victory; and the Lord God will wipe away tears from off all faces; and the rebuke of his people shall he take away from off all the earth; for the Lord hath spoken it. And it shall be said in that day, Lo, this is our God; we have waited for him, and he will save us: this is the Lord; we have waited for him, we will rejoice in his salvation."

Think of it! The redeemed will live throughout eternity without ever seeing death.

* * *

What will life in heaven be like? A partial answer is found in Isaiah 65:21 where we read: "And they shall build houses and inhabit them; and they shall plant vineyards, and eat the fruit of them." Isaiah here teaches us that God will make sure that we will be happily and contentedly occupied. Heaven will be so wonderful that we find in Isaiah 64:4: "For since the beginning of the world men have not heard, nor perceived by the ear, neither hath the eye seen, O God, beside thee, what he hath prepared for him that waiteth for him."

Will it be possible to be happy if separated eternally from loved ones? This is a problem that has puzzled millions of people. The Scripture makes it plain that we will not remember any of the lost, or former things of this world. Notice these words found in Isaiah 65:17: "For, behold, I create new heavens and a new earth: and the former shall not be remembered, nor come into mind."

Our eyes and thoughts will be directed Godward, not earth-ward, forward not backward. Our loved ones who will be lost will undoubtedly be classed with the former things that will not be remembered nor come into mind.

God in His lovingkindness is going to blot out of our minds all things that would tend toward making us unhappy in heaven. In other words, all that will be in heaven will be happy. They will remember all of the good things but none of the bad things. Happi-ness will be the first rule of heaven.

*   *   *

True religion must be learned here on earth. How can we sing the songs of Zion there unless we learn its accents here? In a godly, Israelitish home a group of persons were seated about a phonograph. Among them was a very old, pious man who had never before heard the wonderful little instrument. At first, light tunes only were played. The old man's face showed his astonishment. At length the instrument turned to the songs of Israel and strange, wonderful voices from far away, yet also very near, were heard singing the strains of the faith of Israel. The old man moved his chair closer, lost to all about him. At length a sweet voice was heard singing:

> *Eli, Eli, lo-mo a sav-to-ni?*
>   *Eli, Eli lo-mo a-sav-to-ni?*
> In fire and flame everywhere they burned us
> Persecuted, disgraced and ever made to suffer,
> Yet none succeeded to turn us from Thee,
> From thee my God—and from thy sacred Torah,
>   from thy Command
> *Eli lo-mo a-sav-toni?*
>   *Eli, Eli lo-mo a-sav-to-ni?*
> Day and night, my guide
> Thy light with reverence supreme I guard with awe.
> Thy sacred law, O my Lord,
> Save me now, O spare me once again
> As thou dist thy children in days of yore.
> Hear thou, O Lord my lamentation.
> Thou Alone art my salvation.
> Hear Israel, Our Lord is our God, Our Lord is One!

Then the old man's self-restraint broke down utterly, and forget-ting his feebleness, ignoring his broken voice and the presence of the company, he joined in the song, joyous at the nearness and preciousness of God. He had already learned the songs of Zion, and when he heard voices singing them they were not new songs to him, but old and dear. If we learn to make melody in the heart here, we shall have no difficulty in singing the heavenly strains there.

The wonders of heaven are beyond all human comprehension. The Lord says that:

"The wolf and the lamb feed together, and the lion shall eat straw like the bullock: and dust shall be the serpent's meat. They shall not hurt nor destroy in all my holy mountain saith the Lord" (Isaiah 65:25).

"The wolf also shall dwell with the lamb, and the leopard shall lie down with the kid; and the calf and the young lion and the fatling together; and a little child shall lead them" (Isaiah 11:6).

No artist has ever been able to paint a picture, nor has he ever been able to comprehend the beauties of heaven as they actually are. Human minds are inadequate to comprehend the marvels and splendors that await us. Concerning this we read in Psalm 31:19: "Oh how great is thy goodness, which thou hast laid up for them that fear thee; which thou hast wrought for them that trust in thee before the sons of men!"

*   *   *

The story is told of a boy who was born blind in 1928. It was observed that he had cataracts but the doctor said that he could not operate on him until he was about eighteen years of age. In 1938 his father took him to an eye specialist to have surgery for his cataracts. The operation was successful and when the day arrived to remove the bandages the boy was taken into a dimly lighted room. He sat in a chair while the nurse unwrapped the bandages from his eyes. His father was seated on one side watching and the doctor was seated on the other side.

When the last bandage was removed, the young man looked into the nurse's face and said, "Nurse! I can see! You are beautiful and your eyes seem to sparkle. Tell me, nurse, do your eyes really sparkle?" She answered, "Yes, everyone's eyes sparkle." Then he looked at the man sitting at his right, and said, "Who is this sitting at my right?" The man began, "I am—" but the boy interrupted and said, "Doctor, I recognize your voice. Oh, how thankful I am to you that now I can see!" Then looking to his left, he said, "Who is this sitting here?" The man started, "I am—" but he was interrupted by the boy who said, "Dad, I recognize your voice. I am so happy I can see," and then he dropped his head and began to cry. The father stood up and put his arms around the boy and said, "Son, why are you crying? I thought you were happy." He answered, "Yes, Dad, I am happy that I can see, but oh, how I wish that

Mother had lived so that I now could see her." The father said, "Son, I knew that you would probably want to see what your mother looked like, so I brought along a picture of your mother and you look just like her." The boy looked at the picture and then his father handed him a mirror, and as he looked at the picture and the mirror he said, "Dad, you are right, I do look like Mother."

One year later he was interviewed by reporters of the various press associations and was asked what was the most wonderful thing in his life after he could see, and this was his answer: "For the first six months I could not believe that this world was so beautiful. The beauties of this world so fascinated me that I thought I would lose my mind because of overjoy." He then was asked what was the most beautiful in this world, and he replied, "Color." He said that he had never dreamed nor had it ever entered into his mind that color was so beautiful. He had always thought of it as being like our conception of a black and white picture with its contrasts and highlights. He said that the beauties of the various colored flowers; the red, orange, yellow, violet, blue, and green fascinated him beyond all human imagination. He said that everything in this world was more beautiful than his wildest imagination. That is the way heaven will appear to all of us.

In Psalm 32:11 we read: "Be glad in the Lord, and rejoice, ye righteous...."

Then we will realize the words written in Isaiah 64:4: "For since the beginning of the world men have not heard, nor perceived by the ear, neither hath the eye seen, O God, beside thee, what he hath prepared for him that waiteth for him."

Even so come, Lord Jesus.

14

The Power of Prayer

THE POWER OF PRAYER

The past several decades have been of unprecedented tragedy for mankind. They opened with a series of bloody pogroms of Hitler, and now we have the Communists' scourge. As the second half century proceeds, we are, individually and collectively, confronted with grave and frustrating problems. Theologians sense the impact of these uncertain and troublous times, and wonder what the future may have in store.

In such a time as this we may well inquire, "Whence shall my help come?" (Psalms 121:1 A.S.V.). Indeed, to whom can we look for help in this late hour? Who will plead our cause? Is human help adequate to meet such a crisis as the world faces today? There are sorrows which no human balm can soothe, heartaches which no human psychologist can heal, or antibiotic can reach.

In such a time as this we must look to a source infinitely higher than man, to a power excelling that of the mightiest potentates and governments of earth. It is God, and God alone, who can help, and who will help us in answer to our solemn, sincere, heartfelt prayer.

By prayer we mean the spontaneous cry of the soul to God, with the full assurance that: "The righteous cry, and the Lord heareth, and delivereth them out of all their troubles" (Psalm 34:17).

True heartfelt prayer has been likened to a key in the hand of faith that unlocks heaven's storehouse, wherein are treasured the boundless resources of grace.

*　　*　　*

We must learn to pray like Abraham, who pleaded the cause of the remnant of righteous people left in Sodom! We must pray like

159

Moses, who offered to have his own name blotted from the Book of Life if that could be the means of saving Israel from destruction! We must learn to supplicate our heavenly Father like Elijah, whose prayer brought fire down from heaven and consumed the sacrifice! We must utter prayers that will rend heaven and move the arm of the Almighty.

Such prayer changes things! Take the experience of David, for example. In the hour of utmost extremity, when the waters of affliction passed over his soul and seemed about to engulf him, when he despaired of his very life, he looked to God for help. Read his inspiring utterance in Psalm 121:1, 2. "I will lift up mine eyes unto the hills, from whence cometh my help. My help cometh from the Lord, which made heaven and earth."

And again: "the salvation of the righteous is of the Lord: he is their strength in the time of trouble. And the Lord shall help them and deliver them: he shall deliver them from the wicked, and save them, because they trust in him" (Psalms 37:39, 40).

Did God honor David's prayer? Those of us who are familiar with sacred history know that God heard the prayers of David and in a most singular manner delivered him out of his distresses.

When Israel engaged in mortal combat with the Amalekites, a fierce, warlike tribe, it was observed that: "when Moses held up his hand, that Israel prevailed: and when he let down his hand, Amalek prevailed" (Exodus 17:11).

True faith and true prayer—how strong they are! They are as two strong arms by which the human suppliant lays hold upon the power of Infinite Love. As the Hebrews triumphed when Moses stretched out his hands to heaven for help and intercession in behalf of Israel, so may also the Christians of today prevail when they, by faith and prayer, take hold upon the strength and power of the mighty Holy Spirit.

*   *   *

Some ask, Will God display His mighty power and perform His great wonders today as He did in behalf of His people anciently? Ask the hero of Guadalcanal, Charlie Ross, and he will tell you what prayer did for him. It saved him from certain death!

Or, ask Captain Eddie Rickenbacker, and his six companions who were stranded in the Pacific, and drifted aimlessly on a shoreless sea, in rubber rafts, for twenty-six days. They languished from heat, hunger, and thirst, and their prospect of being saved was negligible from the human standpoint. Yet their united prayers for divine help brought food, sweet water, and finally complete deliverance.

Had it not been for the above harrowing experience, some of the men adrift might never have learned of the efficacy of true prayer, or what a present help God can be in time of trouble. You have undoubtedly read the following testimony of Lieutenant James G. Whittaker, co-pilot of the Rickenbacker plane:

"For me those blazing days represent the greatest adventure a man can have—the one in which he finds his God. We met as strangers in the watery wastes along the equator. We might have remained strangers.

"I was an agnostic; an atheist, if you will. But from my companions *I learned to pray. I saw prayer answered.* There are no atheists in the foxholes of Guadalcanal, and *there can be no atheists in rubber rafts amid whitecaps and sharks.* My entire life has been changed by the events that began October 20, 1942. It is a day I'll never forget."

* * *

It must not, however, be assumed because of the above experiences that every prayer will be answered unconditionally. There are certain conditions with which we must comply before God will hear and answer our prayers.

One of the first of these is that we feel our need of help from Him. He has promised: "I will pour water upon him that is thirsty, and floods upon the dry ground" (Isaiah 44:3).

Those who hunger and thirst after righteousness, who long after Jesus, may be sure that their prayers will be heard and answered. The heart must be open to the Spirit's influence, or God's blessing cannot be received. Our need is itself an argument, and pleads most eloquently in our behalf. But we must ask the Lord Jesus to do these things for us. He says, "Ask, and it shall be given you."

Another condition of effectual prayer is to hate sin. The inspired Psalmist declares: "If I regard iniquity in my heart, the Lord will not hear me" (Psalm 66:18).

If we cling to any known sin, and willfully violate the love of God, the answer to our petition will be delayed until all wrongs have been made right. For example, for twenty years Jacob's life was embittered by doubt, perplexity, and remorse, because of his sin against his brother Esau. Wrestling all night in prayer by the brook Jabbok, he repented of his sin and was forgiven. In his night of anguish, when destruction seemed just ahead, Jacob learned how vain is the help of man, how groundless is all trust in human power. As he turned to the divine favor, his name was changed from Jacob, a "supplanter," to Israel, "a prince of God." Having thus effectually prevailed with God in prayer, he was also able to prevail with his brother Esau.

In the days of Daniel, the prophet, a national catastrophe had overtaken the children of Israel because of their continual backsliding. The mighty hordes of Babylonia were permitted to invade their land. Many were carried captive to live in servitude to Nebuchadnezzar and to his sons, "until the reign of the kingdom of Persia." Then the prophet Daniel besought the Lord's favor in behalf of Jerusalem which lay desolate, and in behalf of repentant Israel. His was no self-righteous prayer, but confessing their sins as his own, he plead: "We have sinned, and have committed iniquity, and have done wickedly, and have rebelled, even by departing from thy precepts and from thy judgments: Neither have we hearkened unto thy servants the prophets" (Daniel 9:5, 6).

God heard the prayer of Daniel. The heart of their captors was profoundly moved with the determination to free the Judean captives and to help them restore the temple of God. Thus again, the effectual prayer of a righteous man availed much.

Let the people of today beseech the Lord with the same deep heartsearching that made so effectual the prayer of illustrious leaders of old; yes, let us pray in the spirit of David, of Jacob, and of Daniel, and we shall not pray in vain.

Did God forget faithful Noah when judgments were visited upon the antediluvian world? Did He forget Lot when fire came down from heaven to consume the cities of the plain? Did He forget Joseph surrounded by idolaters in Egypt? Did He forget Elijah when the oath of Jezebel threatened him with the fate of the prophets of Baal? Did He forget Jeremiah in the dark and dismal pit of his prison-house? Did he forget the three Hebrew stalwarts in the fiery furnace, or Daniel in the den of lions? To every earnest seeker who is conscious of his own unworthiness, who seeks God with genuine humility and deep contrition, is given this blessed assurance: "The Lord is nigh unto them that are of a broken heart; and saveth such as be of a contrite spirit" (Psalm 34:18).

Still another condition of effectual prayer is faith; that is to say, we must have implicit confidence in what God has promised in His word. We are assured that, "The eyes of the Lord are upon the righteous, and his ears are open unto their cry" (Psalm 34:15). Why not take God at His word?

When we do not receive the very things for which we ask, at the time we ask, we are still to believe that the Lord hears, and that He will answer our prayers. We are so erring and short-sighted that we sometimes ask for things that would not be a blessing to us, and our heavenly Father in love answers our prayers by giving us that which will be for our highest good—that which we ourselves would desire if with vision enlightened we could see all things as they really are. When our prayers seem not to be answered, we are to cling to the promise; for the time of answering will surely come, and we shall receive the blessing we need most. But to claim that prayer will always be answered in the very way and for the particular thing that we desire, is false presumption. God is too wise to err, and too good to withhold any good thing from them that walk uprightly. Therefore you do not see the immediate answer to your prayers. But through it all rely upon His sure promise: "Ask and it shall be given you."

Let the soul of man be drawn out and upward, that God may grant us a breath of the heavenly atmosphere. Let us keep so near to God that in every unexpected trial our thoughts will turn to Him as naturally as a body of water engulfs the rain.

* * *

This is an age of distress of nations with bewilderment, as was predicted by the prophets. This state of uncertainty has affected all nations, and has, to a greater or lesser degree, touched the lives of all America. There are many troubled people today; many whose hearts have been torn by separation, or perhaps by the loss of loved ones on the battlefield. Millions are distressed because of the indescribable suffering that exists in the world today. Men's hearts are literally failing them for fear, and for looking after those things which are coming on the earth. And, indeed what man is there whose courage and faith are not being tested in these tumultuous and troublous times? Perhaps this era finds *you* discouraged and fearful of what the morrow may bring. Or it may be that you have suffered financial reverses, and find that your spirit is well-nigh crushed by the everyday burdens and uncertainties that seem to be your lot. Your associates may prove untrue, and life may seem to hold but little that is worth living and struggling for. In your utter helplessness you may feel alone and forsaken, with no one who understands or cares.

Be of good cheer; there is a solution for every problem that may confront you; there is a balm in Gilead for every aching heart. You are not left alone to struggle against apparently insurmountable obstacles. Through prayer you may come in contact with the great Powerhouse of the universe, even your heavenly Father, who has a thousand ways of helping you of which you know nothing.

The Army and Navy files contain records that tell how men in dire distress on land, at sea, and in the air, have received divine aid in answer to their earnest prayer for help. Yes, God can indeed change, wonderfully change, the most hopeless, discouraging outlook as you trust in the lovingkindness of the Lord Jesus and accept in faith God's promise that "all things work together for good to them that love God." Even your disappointed hopes and your seemingly unanswered prayers will, in the future life, be seen in their true perspective, and then be recognized as among your greatest blessings.

The Lord is full of pity and of tender mercy. His heart of love is touched by our sorrows, and even by our utterances of them. Take to Jesus everything that perplexes the mind. There is no chapter in our experience too dark for Him to read; there is no perplexity too difficult for Him to unravel. No calamity can befall the least of His children, no anxiety harass the soul, no joy or cheer, no sincere prayer escape the lips, of which our heavenly Father is unobservant, or in which He takes no immediate interest. "He healeth the broken in heart, and bindeth up their wounds."

*　　*　　*

If those suffering from bodily infirmities would believe in the efficacy of prayer, many would doubtless be healed of their diseases and be restored to health. However, we need to guard against those cults whose chief drawing power is their claim to so-called "divine healing." Many place their confidence in charlatans and "magnetic healers" as though there were no Great Physician or loving heavenly Father "Who forgiveth all thine iniquities; who healeth all thy diseases" (Psalm 103:3).

After praying for healing, we still have a duty to perform. We should remove every hindering factor that would prevent the granting of our petition.

Many of us bring disease upon ourselves by constant self-indulgence. We do not live in accordance with God's natural law or the principles of holy living. Others disregard the laws of sanitation in their habits of eating and drinking. Often some form of vice is the cause of feebleness of mind and body. Should these persons gain the blessing of health, many of them would continue to pursue the same course of heedless transgression of God's physical and spiritual laws, reasoning that if God heals them in answer to prayer, they are at liberty to continue their unlawful practices and to indulge perverted appetite without restraint. If God were to work a miracle in restoring these persons to health, He would be encouraging sin. In order to receive His blessing in answer to prayer, they must cease to do evil and learn to do well.

We have the sanction of God's Word for the use of remedial agencies, even after we have prayed for healing. When Hezekiah, king of Israel, was sick and was told by the prophet Isaiah that he was about to die, the monarch pleaded with God that his life might be spared. "Then came the word of the Lord to Isaiah saying, Go, and say to Hezekiah, Thus saith the Lord, the God of David thy father, I have heard thy prayer, I have seen thy tears; behold, I will add unto thy days fifteen years" (Isaiah 38:4, 5).

God had the power to heal Hezekiah instantly, but He chose to use natural means to bring about the desired result. The following directions were given: "Let them take a lump of figs, and lay it for a plaster upon the boil, and he shall recover" (verse 21).

In the healing of king Hezekiah, and of many other afflicted men, women, and children, as recorded in the Scripture, we have multiplied evidence that the God whom we serve delights to help us and to heal our diseases, when it is for our good and to His glory for Him to do so.

*   *   *

So let us thank God for the privilege of prayer. No longer need we be weighted down with cares and frustrations; no longer need sorrow overwhelm us, nor heavy burdens oppress and crush our drooping spirits, as long as we have recourse to the "secret place of the Most High." The God who answered the disciples' prayers and delivered them out of their distresses, bids us: "Fear thou not; for I am with thee:...I will strengthen thee; yea, I will help thee; yea, I will uphold thee with the right hand of my righteousness" (Isaiah 41:10).

King David had implicit confidence and trust in God's guidance and overruling providences. Read his testimony in Psalm 23:4: "Yea, though I walk through the valley of the shadow of death, I will fear no evil: for thou art with me; thy rod and thy staff they comfort me."

And so let us cast our burden upon the Lord, Jesus, and He shall sustain us. As we call upon Him in the day of trouble, the Lord assures us: "I will deliver thee and thou shalt glorify me" (Psalm 50:15).

Prayer is the soul's sincere desire
Uttered or unexpressed;
The motion of a hidden fire
That trembles in the breast.

Prayer is the burden of a sigh,
The falling of a tear,
The upward glancing of an eye,
When none but God is near.

Prayer is the simplest form of speech
That infant lips can try;
Prayer the sublimest strains that reach
The Majesty on high.

Prayer is the contrite sinner's voice,
Returning from his ways;
While angels in their songs rejoice
And cry, "Behold, he prays!"

Prayer is the Christian's vital breath,
The Christian's native air,
His watchword at the gates of death;
He enters heaven with prayer.

O Thou, by whom we come to God,
The Life, the Truth, the Way;
The path of prayer thyself hast trod:
Lord, teach us how to pray!

—JAMES MONTGOMERY.

15

The Temple and Sacrifices

THE TEMPLE AND SACRIFICES

The fast of the fifth Jewish month, called *Tisha B'av,* has much sadness and sorrow associated with it. Every midsummer, on the 9th day of the month of *Av,* pious Jews the world over observe the anniversary of the destruction of the second temple. Although the burning of that magnificent temple occurred nearly two milleniums ago, time cannot entirely eradicate or efface that terrible tragedy from the heart and memory of the Hebrew people. What a never-to-be forgotten catastrophe that must have been, to cause a whole nation to bemoan and lament to this very day that which happened nearly twenty centuries ago.

But weeping and abstaining from food will not heal the wound of centuries. No amount of fasting will restore the temple. If comfort of any kind can at all be derived from this tragic experience, it is that we of this age may profit from the unfortunate mistakes of another day, by inquiring into the underlying causes that brought about such a fearful national calamity. There is food for thought in the wise man's adage: "The curse causeless shall not come" (Proverbs 26:2).

*　　*　　*

In order to ascertain the cause of that calamity we must have a clear comprehension of God's original purpose in the construction and erection of that glorious temple. When Moses was charged by God to build Him a sanctuary, he was commissioned to carry the following message to the people: "And let them make me a sanctuary; that I may dwell among them (Exodus 25:8).

That sacred temple was designed by God to be the embodiment of a great spiritual truth. It was to reveal to Israel, and through them to the Gentile world, heaven's plan for the redemption of the human race from sin. The services in the temple were also designed to show how the poor repentant sinner can be forgiven.

The Scripture tells us that sin is the transgression of God's law —the Moral Commandments. The reason why the Temple services centered around the holiness of God enshrined in the sacred ark, is because man transgressed that law. And because man broke that law it became necessary for Jehovah to institute the sacrificial system of offerings for the covering of sin. The slaying of the innocent lambs was designed to impress upon the Hebrew people the truth that some day the Saviour, the innocent and undefiled divine Substitute, would come and die in place of the guilty sinner. This Substitute could forgive sins!

The services of this sacrificial system were later transferred to the temple, but they taught the same spiritual lessons, and had the same objective in view. Solomon clearly understood this, as is evident from his letter to Hiram: "And the house which I build is great: for great is our God above all gods. But who is able to build him an house, seeing the heaven and heaven of heavens cannot contain him? who am I then, that I should build him an house, *save only to burn sacrifice before him?*" (II Chronicles 2:5, 6).

Concerning the purpose of the sacrifices, Moses says: "For the life of the flesh is in the blood: and I have given it to you upon the altar to make an atonement for your souls: *for it is the blood that maketh an atonement for the soul*" (Leviticus 17:11).

The language of this Scripture is clear and self-explanatory. The purpose of the shedding of the blood of these innocent animals was that an atonement might be made for the soul, that the sinner might again become "at-one" with God. Sin has erected a tall wall between God and man, as is emphasized in the following Scripture: "Behold, the Lord's hand is not shortened, that it cannot save; neither his ear heavy, that it cannot hear: But your iniquities have separated between you and your God, and your sins have hid his face from you, that he will not hear" (Isaiah 59:1, 2).

*   *   *

The sacrificial system pointed to the Saviour in every respect. The sacrifices were an assurance to repentant sinner that a way had been found whereby he could again be reconciled to his God. Through every sacrifice that was offered, our ever compassionate heavenly Father said of the guilty sinner: "Deliver him from going down to the pit: I have found a ransom [an atonement]" (Job 33:24).

The Saviour is the Ransom. He is the innocent Substitute of whom all the prophets wrote. Every lamb that the sinner brought, expressed the idea of a substitutionary death. We have just read that Moses understood the purpose of the sacrifices. To prophets who followed Moses, this same precious truth concerning substitutionary death was revealed. Note how clearly the illustrious prophet Isaiah speaks of the Saviour as of One who is to suffer in our stead:

"Surely he hath borne *our* griefs, and carried *our* sorrows: yet we did esteem him stricken, smitten of God, and afflicted. But he was wounded for *our* transgressions, He was bruised for *our* iniquities: the chastisement of *our* peace was upon him; and with his stripes *we* are healed. All we like sheep have gone astray; we have turned every one to his own way; and the Lord hath laid on him the iniquity of *us all*. He was oppressed, and he was afflicted, yet he opened not his mouth: he is brought as a *lamb to the slaughter...*" (Isaiah 53:4-7).

When the Saviour appeared, John the Baptist said of Him: "Behold the *Lamb* of God, which taketh away the sin of the world" (John 1:29).

From the foregoing it is clear that all the sacrifices prefigured the Saviour. The offerings of animals were not an end, but a means to an end. They were a type; and the precious Saviour was the Anti-type. They were a shadow, while the Saviour is the Substance.

*   *   *

The Hebrew prophets stated and restated, iterated and reiterated the fact that the sacrificial system was only figurative, and was to end with the coming of the Saviour. We quote from the inspired prophet Daniel: "And He [referring to the Saviour] shall confirm the covenant with many for one week: and in the midst of the week *he shall cause the sacrifice and oblation to cease*" (Daniel 9:27).

The Jewish leaders understood that the animal offerings were to terminate with the coming of the Saviour. One rabbi says: "All sacrifices shall end in the days of the Saviour, except for the sacrifice of thanksgiving" (*Leviticus Misrash Rabba,* Chapter 27, section 12, last part).

The Scriptures declare that the Saviour would appear the first time while the second temple was still standing, as may be seen from the following prophecies:

"For thus saith the Lord of hosts; Yet once, it is a little while.... And I will shake all nations, and *the Desire of all nations shall come:* and I will fill this house [the second temple] with glory, saith the Lord of hosts.... The glory of this latter house shall be greater than the former, saith the Lord of Hosts; and in this place will I give peace, saith the Lord of hosts" (Haggai 2:6-9).

"Behold, I will send my messenger, and he shall prepare the way before me: and *the Lord* [*the Saviour*], *whom ye seek, shall suddenly come to his temple, even the messenger of the covenant, whom ye delight in: behold, he shall come,* saith the Lord of hosts" (Malachi 3:1).

The "Desire of all nations" is none other than the Saviour, Jesus of Nazareth. Oh, that those who claimed to believe these Scriptures had pondered them in their hearts! If they had only borne in mind the divine purpose in the erection of the temple! But they lost sight of the symbolic significance of the sacrifices, and perverted the offerings into a superstitious fetishism, regarding them as possessing something meritorious in *themselves,* until the whole sacred economy became corrupted. We quote:

"...and Jesus went up to Jerusalem. And found in the temple those that sold oxen and sheep and doves, and the changers of money sitting: And when he had made a scourge of small cords, he drove them all out of the temple, and the sheep, and the oxen; and poured out the changers' money, and overthrew the tables; And said unto them that sold doves, Take these things hence; make not my Father's house an house of merchandise" (John 2:13-16).

After Jesus the Saviour appeared at the appointed time, He went in and out for three and a half years among the chosen people of God, healing the sick, raising the dead, and preaching the kingdom of God to all. His words, His works, and His life all testified to His Saviourship; but most of the leaders of Israel rejected Him. They had so perverted the Scriptures by their traditions, that they failed to recognize in Him the One to whom Moses and all the prophets pointed. We read that "He came unto his own, and his own received him not" (John 1:11). They still offered their sacrifices, but rejected the Lamb of God, the Saviour, to whom all these sacrifices pointed. They gloried in the temple, but failed to recognize that "One greater than the temple" was among them. (See Matthew 12:6.) The time had come for the Lord to put an end to the services which had been so grossly perverted. When one of the disciples of Jesus pointed with pride to the buildings of the temple, "Jesus answering said unto him, Seest thou these great buildings? there shall not be left one stone upon another, that shall not be thrown down" (Mark 13:2).

* * *

The sacrificial system terminated at the Saviour's atoning death, the God of heaven indicated by a supernatural sign that type had met antitype and thus the sacrifices were no longer necessary. We read, "Behold, the veil of the temple was rent in twain from the top to the bottom" (Matthew 27:51). The Most Holy place—which was once filled with the *Shekinah,* God's visible presence, was thrown open to the gaze of the multitude. By the rending of the veil which divided the two apartments of the temple, God Himself indicated that the most holy place of the earthly sanctuary was no longer sacred, and that the sacrificial system had come to an abrupt end. The temple itself was finally destroyed in the year A.D. 70 by the Roman army under Titus the Conqueror!

God permitted the destruction of the world's most beautiful temple because its services had outlived their intent and usefulness. The sacrificial system served only as an object lesson, or type, of the Saviour's substitutionary sacrifice. His atoning death automatically nullified those ritual services. The hope of the earth's children, therefore, is no longer bound up with an earthly temple and annual sacrifices.

* * *

But while the death of the Saviour did away with the ceremonial laws and sacrifices of the temple services, it did not abolish the Moral Law of God. Some Christians assume that when Jesus died on the cross, He not only abolished the ceremonial laws and sacrifices which pointed to His death, but that He did away with the moral commandments as well. This assumption is opposed to Jesus' teaching. We quote from the Sermon on the Mount: "Think not that I am come to destroy the [moral] law, or the prophets: I am not come to destroy, but to fulfill. For verily I say unto you, Till heaven and earth pass, *one jot or one tittle* shall in no wise pass from the law, till all be fulfilled" (Matthew 5:17, 18).

The "jot," or *yod,* is the smallest letter of the Hebrew alphabet, and is equal in size to a comma in English punctuation. The "tittle" is a small crown, or flourish, made by hand. Jesus declared that not a jot or a tittle shall ever pass from the law. He thus showed what great regard He had for the immutable law of God.

The Moral Laws are eternal and immutable. As long as *Yahweh* is God it will always be wrong to worship false gods, to bow down to images, to take God's name in vain, to profane His Church, to dishonor father or mother, to kill, to commit adultery, to steal, to bear false witness, and to covet.

The object, purpose, and work of the Moral Law is forcefully indicated in the following Scripture: "But be ye doers of the word, and not hearers only, deceiving your own selves. For if any be a hearer of the word, and not a doer, he is like unto a man beholding his natural face in a glass: For he beholdeth himself, and goeth his way, and straightway forgetteth what manner of man he was. But whoso looketh into the perfect law of liberty, and continueth therein, he being not a forgetful hearer, but a doer of the work, this man shall be blessed in his deed" (James 1:22-25).

In these Scriptures the Moral Law of God is compared to a looking glass. A mirror faithfully reflects the least spot or blemish. Its function is not to cleanse, but to reveal the need of cleansing. After the soap and water have accomplished their purpose, the mirror will reflect the result. In a similar manner the law points out our moral blemishes and sins. "Sin is the transgression of the law" (I John 3:4). The law cannot cleanse us, for that is not its function. *Its purpose is to point out sin.* Doing away with that moral law would no more cleanse us from sin, than would the breaking of a looking glass in order to improve our appearance! The only effective cleansing agency to rid us of sin is the one provided for us by our compassionate, sin-pardoning Saviour. We read: "In that day there shall be a fountain opened to the house of David and to the inhabitants of Jerusalem for sin and for uncleanness" (Zechariah 13:1).

It has been abundantly shown that this "fountain" for cleansing is none other than the Saviour, Jesus. We cannot in our own strength keep God's Commandments. We cannot change our sinful hearts, nor can we purify our thoughts, our desires, or motives. The law cannot accomplish this for us. In fact it demands the death of the transgressor; but the Saviour, our Substitute, died for us in order to pay the penalty for its transgression.

*   *   *

To claim that the Saviour did away with the moral commandments, is to make both Him and the Bible of none effect. If the law had been abolished, there would no longer be such a thing as sin, for "where no law is, there is no transgression" (Romans 4:15). For example, if you were arrested for speeding at the rate of eighty miles per hour when there was no law against it, you would not need the judge's pardon, for you had not broken any law. In like manner, in the spiritual realm where there is no law, there is no transgression, and therefore there is no need of forgiveness. If no forgiveness is necessary, then there is no need of a Substitute and no need of a Saviour. If there is no need of a Saviour then the Scriptures are superfluous, since its central theme is salvation through the Saviour. Thus we can readily see that the erroneous teaching that the moral commandments have been abolished is pernicious, subversive, and destructive to all true religion.

To meet such perverse philosophies, the Scriptures repeatedly stress the immutability of God's Moral Law. (See Psalm 111:7, 8.) In Ecclesiastes 12:13, we are told that the whole duty of man is to "Fear God and keep his commandments." In James 2:8-12 it is stated that all will be judged for the violation of God's moral law. Of those who ignore the claims of that law it is declared: "He that turneth away his ear from hearing the law, even his prayer shall be abomination" (Proverbs 28:9).

The law cannot save; but it is a standard of God's excellence. Some excuse themselves from rendering obedience to the Moral Laws of our God because the Scriptures say in Romans 6:14, "Ye are not under the law, but under grace." To be *"under the law"* signifies that we are breaking the law. When a thief is caught with the goods he is under the iron heel of the law. But when the judge out of the kindness of his heart pardons his transgression of the law, he is *under grace;* that is to say, he receives unmerited grace. This pardon now places him under double obligation to keep the law, lest he disgrace his benefactor. The Bible tells us that "all have sinned, and come short of the glory of God" (Romans 3:23). All, therefore, are in need of grace, or unmerited favor, which the Saviour Jesus alone can give. After we have received His pardoning grace, shall we continually practice sin again? In Romans 6:15 we read, "What then? shall we sin, because we are not under the law, but under grace? *God forbid."*

As has already been stated, the Saviour's death abolished the ceremonial law—the law of sacrifices—which pointed to Him who is the only remedy for sin. The law of ceremonies and the moral law of God are two vastly different laws. The ceremonial law was a temporary measure.

Everything which the temple services foreshadowed was fulfilled in the atoning death of the Saviour. "For even Christ our passover is sacrificed for us" (I Corinthians 5:7). The Saviour's death made redemption an accomplished fact. Type met antitype; substance took the place of the shadows. All who long for power to obey the law of God, whether they be Jew or Gentile, must receive help in God's appointed way through the Saviour.

*   *   *

Anciently when an Israelite sinned he was required to bring an offering and confess his sin over the head of the animal, by placing his hands on the victim, and then slaying the innocent victim. Salvation was an individual matter then, even as it is today. There is now no earthly temple to which we may bring a sacrifice. We must believe and accept the atonement which Jesus had made for us by His death, and then we are assured that: "If we confess our sins, he is faithful and just to forgive us our sins, and to cleanse us from all unrighteousness" (I John 1:9).

The story is told about a preacher who bought a very beautiful white suit. One day he accidentally spilled a chemical dye upon it, and feared that he had ruined it. However, he consulted a chemist friend who offered to take the suit to his plant for experimentation. By the skillful blending of certain chemicals he succeeded in completely eradicating the offensive blotch, and returned it to the owner as dazzlingly white and spotless as it was before. The suit showed no imperfection in color.

In the same manner, Jesus the Saviour, is able to take our lives which are ruined by sin, and transform our ugly characters so that we will reflect His own spotless perfection—and likeness. The Saviour will accomplish this for us, *if we are but willing.*

"Come now, and let us reason together, saith the Lord; though your sins be as scarlet, they shall be as white as snow; though they be red like crimson, they shall be as wool. *If ye be willing and obedient,* ye shall eat the good of the land" (Isaiah 1:18, 19).

16

The New Covenant as Promised

THE NEW COVENANT AS PROMISED

A certain young prince had a strange dream one night. He dreamt that he was engaged in deadly combat with an assailant who was bent on his destruction. The young man put forth almost super-human efforts to extricate himself from the iron-like grip of his antagonist, but to no avail. Anxious to know the identity of his adversary, the youth turned quickly and caught a glimpse of his opponent's countenance. To his great astonishment he recognized in the features of his enemy...*his own face.*

Many of the world's philosophers and truly great intellects agree that the fiercest battles are not those waged on bloody battlefields. They are the hidden conflicts that take place in the soul as it strives towards perfection and victory over inherited and cultivated tendencies to evil.

There are three billion men and women today who are hopefully looking, longing, searching for a most precious treasure—peace of mind, peace of soul. Scores of treaties have been written on inward peace, and multitudes are eagerly perusing these volumes in an unceasing effort to secure for themselves this coveted prize. But, like the proverbial pot of gold, it is always beyond their reach.

The demon of fear which is gnawing at the very vitals of society and poisoning the springs of life, causes men and women to besiege their spiritual advisers, rabbis, ministers, priests, psychiatrists, and so-called "healers," in their search for this rare jewel.

Is this your problem? Do you long for peace of mind, for Heaven's forgiveness, for peace and love in the soul? This coveted prize cannot be attained by the mere exercise of will power; nor can it be secured by some intellectual formula, or by magic. Peace of heart is not something that can be bought or sold over the counter. It cannot be purchased for money.

Yet this previous treasure is accessible to all who will but comply with the conditions. Listen: God offers it to you as a gift, "without money and without price."

The chief obstacle to peace of heart is a little word of three letters: s i n. It is sin, with the accompaniment of guilt and remorse, that robs the soul of peace. Peace means being in harmony with your Maker; it is the precious fruit of obedience to God's immutable justice and holiness. Says the prophet: "O that thou hadst hearkened to my commandments! then had thy peace been as a river, and thy righteousness as the waves of the sea" (Isaiah 48:18). Disobedience to God can never bring true, lasting peace. "There is no peace, saith the Lord, unto the wicked" (Isaiah 48:22).

Since sin is the chief obstacle to our peace of heart it should be our determined purpose to rid our lives of this archenemy. There is many an earnest, sincere, conscientious heart that has engaged in the noble work of subduing the evil inclinations of his own nature, only to find that he has dismally failed in the adventure. Are we among those who tried over and over again, and apparently in vain, to overcome those unlovely and unhappy traits of character that constantly clamor for expression? Are we discouraged at times and tempted to give up the struggle, and to surrender the honorable fight? Or are we haunted by the thought that we are fighting a losing battle in life that will ultimately end in defeat? It is our purpose to help in this conflict, so that we may attain our deserving objective; namely, victory over sin. Such victory brings with it an inner contentment, a lasting satisfaction, and an abiding peace of heart for which millions today are craving, but which cannot be obtained in any other way than God's way.

*   *   *

You ask, "How may such a victory be achieved?" Possibly you are of the opinion that man possesses certain inherent powers with which he can conquer all his evil passions. There is indeed a noticeable trend in modern thought in this direction. Man is today exalted as his own redeemer. In his self-will and self-deception he imagines himself to be the proud possessor of power, which will give him the mastery over self and enable him to overcome all objectionable traits of character. Such a philosophy is a delusion, and may be known by its fruit. Without the help of Jesus, man is no more capable of reaching God's standard of perfection than he is able to lift himself to a higher plateau by his own bootstraps.

Humbling us to the dust, the Scriptures declare: "But we are all as an unclean thing, and all our righteousnesses are as filthy rags" (Isaiah 64:6). "The heart is deceitful above all things, and desperately wicked: who can know it?" (Jeremiah 17:9). "Can the Ethiopian change his skin, or the leopard his spots? Then may ye also do good, that are accustomed to do evil" (Jeremiah 13:23). The beloved apostle Paul, adds the following personal testimony: "For I know that in me (that is, in my flesh,) dwelleth no good thing" (Romans 7:18).

In the experience of Israel following their miraculous deliverance from Egyptian bondage, as well as in man's behavior in this supposedly enlightened age, may be found striking illustrations of the truth of the above Scriptures; namely, that man, in and of himself, has no barrier against sin.

For many long and weary centuries the people of Israel had served as bondmen and bondwomen to the mighty Pharaohs. They were utterly powerless to free themselves from their galling yoke of cruel servitude. But in answer to their despairing cries and agonizing tears, God interceded in their behalf and plagued the Egyptians. Having been afflicted by the avenging hand of Israel's God, Pharaoh was forced to release the captives and ultimately set them free.

In his providence God permitted the children of Israel to be brought before the Red Sea with apparently no way of escape from Pharaoh's pursuing hosts in order that He might the more signally manifest His mighty power in their deliverance. When the Egyptians pursued the hosts of Israel through the Red Sea, they were overthrown by God's intervening hand and were swallowed up in the black depths of the turbulent waters. He chose this method, so that their confidence in Him might be established and that their trust in Him might be strengthened. Having chosen Israel as His messianic people, God established His covenant with them. We quote: "Now therefore, if ye will obey my voice indeed, and keep my covenant, then ye shall be a peculiar treasure unto me above all people: for all the earth is mine: And ye shall be unto me a kingdom of priests, and an holy nation" (Exodus 19:5, 6). In response, "all the people answered together, and said, All that the Lord hath spoken we will do" (verse 8).

*   *   *

The basis of this covenant was God's expressed will, and the record of this covenant is found in Exodus. After communing with

God on Mount Sinai, "Moses came and told the people all the words of the Lord, and all the judgments: and all the people answered with one voice, and said, All the words which the Lord hath said will we do (Exodus 24:3). This pledge, together with the words of the Lord, were written in a book. Later this covenant was ratified with the blood of burnt offerings and peace offerings, "And he [Moses] took the book of the covenant, and read in the audience of the people." And again they said, "All that the Lord hath said will we do, and be obedient. And Moses took the blood, and sprinkled it on the people, and said, Behold the blood of the covenant, which the Lord hath made with you concerning all these words" (Exodus 24:7-8).

It should be noted that while the people readily entered into covenant with God they were wholly unaware of the exceeding sinfulness of their own hearts. In pledging "all that the Lord hath said will *we* do," they displayed their self-righteousness and their confidence in their own ability to keep God's righteous desire for them. They did not sense their need of divine transformation.

Soon after, Moses was instructed to build a sanctuary or tabernacle, in order that God might dwell among them. (See Exodus 25:8.) The children of Israel were now fully established as God's peculiar people, with the Holy one of Israel as their king. Had they remained obedient to God's great desire for them, they would have remained the head, and not have become the tail, among the nations of earth. God would have mightily wrought through them for the blessing and uplifting of mankind as promised to Abraham.

But, Israel did not long remain true to their vow. Within a few weeks they broke their covenant with God and bowed down to a golden calf. This was but the beginning of Israel's long history of backsliding, which ended with their subjugation: first, of the northern ten tribes of the kingdom of Israel by Assyria, and later, of the southern kingdom of Judah by Babylon. The people failed miserably to keep their pledge because they trusted in false gods instead of relying on the mighty arm of God.

*   *   *

Since Israel broke the old covenant, God announced through the prophet Jeremiah that He would make a *new covenant* with His people. We quote: "Behold, the days come, saith the Lord, that I will make a *new covenant* with the house of Israel, and with the house of Judah:

"Not according to the covenant that I made with their fathers in the day that I took them by the hand to bring them out of the land of Egypt; which my covenant they brake, although I was an husband unto them, saith the Lord:

"But this shall be the covenant that I will make with the house of Israel; After those days, saith the Lord, I will put my law in their inward parts, and write it in their hearts; and will be their God, and they shall be my people" (Jeremiah 31:31-33).

"In that he saith, A *new* covenant, he hath made the first *old*" (Hebrews 8:13). From these Scriptures we are given to understand that the new covenant was "a *better* covenant, which was established upon *better* promises. "For if that first covenant had been faultless, then should no place have been sought for the second. For finding fault *with them.* he saith, behold, the days come, saith the Lord, when I will make a new covenant with the house of Israel and with the house of Judah" (Hebrews 8:6-8). Thus God declares that the weakness of the old covenant was due to *"them"*; that is, it was due to their self-reliance for victory over sin, instead of seeking the blood of the Messiah, from whom cometh our salvation.

In what respect is the new covenant "better" than the old? Observe that it is established upon "better *promises."* Whereas under the old covenant *Israel* promised to keep the law, under the new covenant it is *God* who makes Himself responsible for the achievement of this objective. Under the new covenant *God* promises the following:

He will put His law in their inward parts.

He will write His law in their hearts.

He will forgive their iniquity, and remember their sins no more.

He will be their God, and they shall be His people.

He will be known to all, to the least as well as to the greatest of them. (This includes the Gentiles as well.)

The purpose, the objective of the new covenant is the same as that of the old, namely, the justification of the sinner by blood! The difference between the two covenants lies in the method for the accomplishment of this objective.

The exceeding marvelous and precious promises embodied in the new covenant, are: pardon for sin, and complete victory over besetting sin. When these have become an accomplished reality in the life of the believer, it creates a oneness between himself and God and *forever* links him with the Eternal One. Should not every heart be everlastingly grateful for this gracious provision? Should not we make this new covenant a choice theme for our meditation and theology?

Yet modern rabbinical Judaism is strangely silent concerning this new covenant: No sermons are preached regarding it; no comments are made with reference to it. Nothing is said about it in the synagogues on Sabbath mornings after the weekly *sedre,* when the *Haftarah* is read. What a singular oversight! What an extraordinary omission! More than twenty-six centuries have rolled by since this promise of a new covenant was made by our God through Jeremiah the prophet. The Hebrew word for covenant is *Brith,* which also means testament. Has God failed to make good His promise to give the children of earth a new covenant? That is impossible, for the Scriptures assure us that "God is not slack concerning His promise," for all His promises are "yea and amen," that is, sure and steadfast. What God has promised He is fully able to perform. Millions today find this new covenant revealed and made plain in the New Testament which is printed in hundreds of languages. Here is eloquent testimony that God has fulfilled His promise of a new covenant which He made through Jeremiah the prophet and fulfilled in Jesus of Nazareth.

*   *   *

When Jesus the Saviour met with his Apostles in an upper chamber to observe His last Passover supper with them, the record states that: "he [Jesus] took the cup, and gave thanks, and gave it to them, saying, Drink ye all of it; For this is my blood of the new testament, which is shed for many for the remission of sins" (Matthew 26:27, 28).

From the time of Jeremiah the prophet until the advent of the Saviour there was an interval of six hundred years. It took six centuries before the promise of a new covenant or testament was fulfilled. The above incident "in an upper chamber" is the first time that the "new testament" is mentioned since Jeremiah's day. In fulfillment of this old testament prediction, Jesus made a new testament with His disciples, every one of whom was a literal descendant of Jacob, from whose loins the people of Israel sprang. Seven hundred years before Jesus was born the prophet Isaiah foretold the divine Saviour's sufferings and work: "But he was wounded for our transgressions, he was bruised for our iniquities: the chastisement of our peace was upon him; and with his stripes we are healed. All we like sheep have gone astray; we have turned every one to

his own way; and the Lord hath laid on him the iniquity of us all
...he is brought as a *lamb* to the slaughter" (Isaiah 53:5-7).

This prophecy was fulfilled by Jesus—the Lamb of God—the day
after He gave the disciples the cup to drink. This cup represented
as symbol His blood which was to be "shed for many for the remission of sins." Indeed, it is only through the blood of Jesus the
Saviour that the forgiveness promised under the new covenant is
made possible. As stated earlier, after Moses ratified the old
covenant with blood, he wrote the record of it in a book. So, likewise, after Jesus ratified the new covenant with His blood, it was
also recorded in a book called the New Testament. Both, the old
and the new covenants are the precious legacy of God's promises to
us. Both testaments have been written and were first circulated by
Jews to the earth's remotest bounds as intended.

All the exceeding great and precious promises embodied in the
new covenant are gloriously fulfilled through Jesus, the Mediator
of the new covenant. (Read Hebrews 8:6.) It is through the divine
power of Jesus that the old, perverse, wicked, and sinful nature is
changed, and that the will of God is inscribed on the pages of the
heart. He it is who enables all who accept Him as their Redeemer
and Mediator of the new covenant, to walk in newness of life. The
Saviour dwelling in the heart of the believer gives him power to
repel every assault of Satan, the archenemy of heart and soul. Then
look no longer to self as the source of strength for victory over sin
and for power to obey God's divine will, but rather unto Jesus who
is "mighty to save" (Isaiah 63:1).

*   *   *

The following parable of deep human interest is given by the
Saviour to illustrate the practical effect of both the old and new
covenants upon the hearts of man. "And he spake this parable unto
certain which trusted in themselves that they were righteous, and
despised others: Two men went up into the temple to pray; the one
a Pharisee, and the other a publican. The Pharisee stood and
prayed thus with himself, God, I thank thee, that I am not as other
men are, extortioners, unjust, adulterers, or even as this publican.
I fast twice in the week. I give tithes of all that I possess. And the
publican, standing afar off, would not lift up so much as his eyes
unto heaven, but smote upon his breast, saying, God be merciful
to me a sinner. I tell you, this man went down to his house justified
rather than the other: for every one that exalteth himself shall be

abased; and he that humbleth himself shall be exalted" (Luke 18:9-14).

Both the Pharisee and the publican (a tax gatherer), were Jews; both believed in the same God; both went to the same house of worship to pray, and yet they were as dissimilar in their attitudes and theologies as were Cain and Abel. The Pharisee trusted in his own merits and righteousness, whereas the publican recognized his spiritual poverty, and in his soul's deep need cried out for help to Him who is "merciful and gracious, longsuffering, and abundant in goodness and truth." (See Exodus 34:6.)

These two men represent the two classes of worshippers. The Pharisee represents the class of professed religionists who boast of their own righteousness and good works. Whether they know it or not, all such act just as did Israel under the old covenant, and belong to the "we will do" category of people. Like the Pharisee, they boast of their good deeds while the heart is still unchanged. Those of this class trust, not in the omnipotent power of their mighty Reedemer, but in meritorious acts or in the observance of laws to attain righteousness and perfection of character. All such expectations will dissipate into nothingness and end in failure and eternal loss. There is only one kind of righteousness which is the righteousness which is imputed to every sincere, contrite sinner who by faith looks unto the Saviour for the fulfillment of all the new covenant promises.

The humble publican, who smote his breast saying: "God be merciful to me a sinner" and who, as Jesus assures us, went home justified (was accounted righteous) represents those who trust not in themselves, but in the merits and righteousness of Jesus the Saviour who is "the Lord of righteousness."

Never can we hope to extricate ourselves from these enslaving fetters, nor can we enjoy peace of heart as long as we are held in bondage by the chains of our own sinful habits. The Bible, speaking of the strife in the heart, says: "For the good that I would, I do not: but the evil which I would not, that I do....O wretched man that I am! who shall deliver me from the body of this death?" (Romans 7:19, 24).

*   *   *

Our heavenly Father did not wait for an emergency call from this sin-infested world. The sight of human wretchedness stirred all heaven to activity in man's behalf. After Adam and Eve yielded to the vile tempter and disobeyed the Lord's express command, they hid themselves "from the presence of the Lord," but the compassionate heavenly Father sought them out. "And the Lord called unto Adam and said unto him, *"Where art thou?"* It was after this that the Lord announced to Adam the good news of a Redeemer to come. Man did not seek God; the plan for his rescue is not of human origin. It springs from the depths of the Father's great heart of love.

To effect our rescue from the snares of the evil one, the Saviour was willing to drink the cup of woe and sorrow, and to suffer every infamy, insult, and agony that the master mind of Satan could invent. Having overcome the archenemy of God and man, Jesus now sits at the right hand of God. "Wherefore he is able also to save them to the uttermost that come unto God by him, seeing he ever liveth to make intercession for them" (Hebrews 7:25). Dear friend, the Saviour is the only source of your strength in your battle with sin.

During World War II, when our boys languished in the enemy's prison camps around the world and our brave and gallant soldiers and sailors risked their lives in order to rescue them from their prolonged torture and living death, do you not think that the hearts of these freed Americans and Allies overflowed with boundless love and gratitude to their deliverers?

Being captivated by the Devil by nature, we are like the children born in Europe's internment camps who never knew the thrill of freedom until they were delivered. It is only as we experience the glorious freedom from sin through the power of the New Birth, that we appreciate how precious is the salvation which is within our reach under the blessings of the new covenant.

Our compassionate Redeemer came from heaven's peaceful realm down to this sin-cursed world, the territory of the Prince of darkness in order that He might deliver us from the prisonhouse of sin and death. This rescue cost our Saviour His precious life, because it was the only means of overcoming our cruel and merciless foe.

Is it any wonder that some day the freed captives of the Devil— a multitude which no man can number—standing before God's throne in His eternal and glorious kingdom, will express with resounding musical voices their undying gratitude and praise: "Blessing, and honor, and glory, and power, be unto him that sitteth upon the throne, and unto the Lamb for ever and ever" (Revelation 5:13).

The freedom from the thraldom of sin is one of the precious fruits of the new covenant. Through faith in Jesus the age-old personal problem of sin is solved; and when this great problem is solved, all the other problems are likewise settled. The precious Saviour and Redeemer is able and eager to deliver you from the sin which does so easily beset you. But you too have a responsibility. You have to accept this proffered help, and yield your will to Him, pledging from henceforth to serve and obey Him as Lord and Saviour.

As you do this you will enjoy a peace of mind that passes all understanding; and to you will be fulfilled the precious promise: *"Peace* I leave with you, my *peace* I give unto you: not as the world giveth, give I unto you. Let not your heart be troubled, neither let it be afraid" (John 14:27).

"Thou wilt keep him in *perfect peace,* whose mind is stayed on thee: because he trusteth in thee" (Isaiah 26:3).

TEXTUAL INDEX

The Old Testament is filled with good news. Long ago it was said that in the Old Testament the New Testament lay concealed and in the New Testament the Old Testament was revealed. The author of this book helps us to see this with force and clarity through the following chapters:

Anyone interested in enlarging and deepening his spiritual life through an increased knowledge of Scripture will enjoy and profit from the reading of this book. Ministers will here find a wealth of material for sermons. This book may well be used in courses on the Bible in Bible schools and colleges.